SO-BWA-470

**New Directions for
Institutional Research**

Robert K. Toutkoushian
EDITOR-IN-CHIEF

J. Fredericks Volkwein
ASSOCIATE EDITOR

Applying Economics to Institutional Research

Robert K. Toutkoushian
Michael B. Paulsen
EDITORS

Number 132 • Winter 2006
Jossey-Bass
San Francisco

APPLYING ECONOMICS TO INSTITUTIONAL RESEARCH
Robert K. Toutkoushian, Michael B. Paulsen (eds.)
New Directions for Institutional Research, no. 132
Robert K. Toutkoushian, Editor-in-Chief

NEW DIRECTIONS FOR INSTITUTIONAL RESEARCH (ISSN 0271-0579, electronic ISSN 1536-075X) is part of The Jossey-Bass Higher and Adult Education Series and is published quarterly by Wiley Subscription Services, Inc., A Wiley Company, at Jossey-Bass, 989 Market Street, San Francisco, California 94103-1741 (publication number USPS 098-830). Periodicals Postage Paid at San Francisco, California, and at additional mailing offices. POSTMASTER: Send address changes to New Directions for Institutional Research, Jossey-Bass, 989 Market Street, San Francisco, California 94103-1741.

SUBSCRIPTIONS cost $80.00 for individuals and $185.00 for institutions, agencies, and libraries in the United States. See order form at end of book.

EDITORIAL CORRESPONDENCE should be sent to Robert K. Toutkoushian, Educational Leadership and Policy Studies, Education 4220, 201 N. Rose Ave., Indiana University, Bloomington, IN 47405.

New Directions for Institutional Research is indexed in College Student Personnel Abstracts, Contents Pages in Education, and Current Index to Journals in Education (ERIC).

Microfilm copies of issues and chapters are available in 16mm and 35mm, as well as microfiche in 105mm, through University Microfilms, Inc., 300 North Zeeb Road, Ann Arbor, Michigan 48106-1346.

www.josseybass.com

CONTENTS

EDITORS' NOTES   1
Robert K. Toutkoushian, Michael B. Paulsen

1. Overview of Economic Concepts, Models, and Methods for   5
Institutional Research
Michael B. Paulsen, Robert K. Toutkoushian
This chapter provides an introduction to economics and how econo-
mists approach their work, and it addresses the relevance of economics
for institutional research.

2. Applying Economics to Institutional Research on Higher   25
Education Revenues
John J. Cheslock
This chapter examines the economic concepts related to how revenues
are generated by institutions of higher education—and how institu-
tional researchers can use this information in their work.

3. Using Economic Concepts in Institutional Research on   43
Higher Education Costs
Paul T. Brinkman
This chapter examines how marginal and average costs, and variable
and fixed costs, are interpreted for colleges and universities and how
these concepts can be used to inform policymaking and institutional
research applications.

4. Using Economic Concepts to Inform Enrollment   59
Management
Stephen L. DesJardins, Allison Bell
This chapter illustrates how economic concepts can be used by insti-
tutional researchers who are involved in the enrollment management
functions at their institutions.

5. Economic Contributions to Institutional Research on   75
Faculty
Robert K. Toutkoushian
This chapter describes how economic theories, models, and reasoning
can help shape institutional research work related to faculty.

6. Economics and Institutional Research: Expanding the Connections and Applications 95

Michael B. Paulsen, Robert K. Toutkoushian

This chapter briefly reviews the key contributions of economics to IR in the past and the present and then provides examples and recommendations for expanding the connections between economics and institutional research through new and/or extended uses of public sector economics in future IR applications.

INDEX 105

EDITORS' NOTES

Education is a unique field in that researchers borrow heavily from many different academic disciplines when conducting their work. A quick glance at the faculty in many education departments would reveal individuals who were trained in such diverse fields as law, sociology, anthropology, business, philosophy, psychology, and history, to name only a few. This is largely a result of the many different types of problems and issues that researchers are confronted with in the education arena.

One area in particular that has the potential to greatly inform our understanding of higher education, and hence institutional research, is the field of economics. People often make the mistake of equating economics with business-related professional disciplines such as finance and accounting, which limits their view on the utility of economics for examining education issues. Economics, however, is a much broader discipline that focuses on any type of problem where entities must make decisions about what to do in the face of constraints on their resources such as time and income. Microeconomics is typically divided into two main areas: how individuals make decisions and how organizations make decisions.

Viewed in this way, there are potentially many different education problems to which economic principles can be applied. Economists look at institutions of higher education as organizations that have to make decisions about which students to enroll, how many students to enroll, how much to pay faculty, and so on. Their decisions are affected by the fact that space is required to accommodate students and revenues are needed to pay faculty. Similarly, students are individuals who must decide whether and how much higher education to obtain, where to receive their education, what courses to take, how much effort to put forth in each class, whether they should stay at their chosen institution or transfer, and how long they should take to complete their studies. Students are constrained, however, in terms of the time that they can devote to education and their ability to pay for it. Faculty are also looked at by economists as individuals who must make decisions about where to work and how to allocate their time between research, teaching, and service.

In this volume of *New Directions for Institutional Research*, we provide an overview of the many ways that economic concepts, models, and methods have been, and can be, applied to higher education problems encountered in institutional research (IR). The volume authors are uniquely qualified to provide this perspective because they are all higher education

NEW DIRECTIONS FOR INSTITUTIONAL RESEARCH, no. 132, Winter 2006 © Wiley Periodicals, Inc.
Published online in Wiley InterScience (www.interscience.wiley.com) • DOI: 10.1002/ir.192

researchers who have received graduate training in economics. In addition, collectively they have substantial experience working directly in IR and thus can appreciate the possible connections between IR work and economics. Throughout the volume, we sought to limit the use of mathematics and equations in presenting economic concepts relevant to IR. Nonetheless, when this could not be avoided, care was taken to provide the intuition behind the approaches being used.

As with any other academic discipline, economics has its own language and ways of approaching problems. Terms such as *opportunity costs, demand, supply, prices, subsidies, marginal costs* and *marginal benefits, comparative statics, constraints, externalities,* and so on have specific meanings to economists and yet are often vague and confusing to noneconomists. Economists also rely heavily on higher-level mathematics including calculus, linear algebra, and statistics in their work. Sometimes these aspects of the field make it difficult for noneconomists to understand and appreciate the methods that economists use. To help in this regard, in the first chapter, Michael Paulsen and Robert Toutkoushian provide an overview of key economic concepts, theories, models, and methods that are useful for understanding the material to be presented in subsequent chapters. Chapter One also presents some of the fundamental and essential concepts and models that are used throughout several of the following chapters. For example, the chapters on higher education revenues (Chapter Two), enrollment management (Chapter Four), and faculty (Chapter Five) all rely heavily on the notion of a demand curve.

In Chapter Two, John Cheslock discusses how economists view the revenues of an institution and how this understanding can be useful for institutional researchers. The federal government recently changed its accounting standards for public institutions to mirror the standards that private institutions use. One of the main changes is to report information on net tuition revenue as compared to gross tuition revenue. This change followed from discussions as to whether the dollars previously categorized as scholarship and fellowship expenditures were truly expenditures or actually a discount on revenues. Chapter Two covers the revenue sources for institutions of higher education and relates these to theories of pricing and institutional behavior.

In particular, Cheslock discusses the important role that subsidies play in higher education finance. Both public and private institutions are highly dependent on subsidies—that is, revenues from various nontuition sources—to help cover some portion of the cost of delivering educational services. In the public sector, states have traditionally provided the largest subsidies in the form of state appropriations. Private institutions, in contrast, rely more heavily on private gifts, grants and contracts, and endowment earnings to help subsidize or offset the costs of providing education. In each instance, the price charged to students in the form of tuition and fees can be thought of as the cost of providing education minus the per-student subsidy from all sources. This economic conceptualization of the relationship among costs, subsidies, and tuition is a particularly useful framework for institutional researchers to understand when they are engaged in discussions with administrators and policymakers about the cause of rising tuition rates, and how to construct performance indicators relating to efficiency.

In Chapter Three on higher education costs, Paul Brinkman focuses on the cost side of the higher education enterprise, that is, how an economist explains the costs that colleges and universities incur in order to provide educational services. As he notes, institutional researchers are uniquely positioned to provide administrators with an understanding of the costs of providing education due to their positions in the administrative hierarchy and their frequent interaction with raw data and data reporting on cost issues for the institution. The economics of costs go well beyond the counting and reporting of expenditures, however, and it is here that significant value added is possible through application of an economic lens. For example, in discussions we have had with administrators, we have found that when they are asked a question like, "How much would it cost to enroll an additional student?" not uncommonly they answer that it was the average cost. However, the marginal cost is a much better construct to use for representing this additional cost; the reason is that many costs, such as library expenditures and administration costs, do not have to increase proportionately when an additional student is enrolled. This distinction can be significant for policymakers to understand, and by applying economic concepts to their work, institutional researchers can help in this regard. Chapter Three addresses the different types of costs in the delivery of higher education services and how economic concepts can be used to understand them. Throughout the chapter, Brinkman relates these concepts and IR to the type of information administrators need.

In Chapter Four, Stephen DesJardins and Allison Bell extend the discussion of revenues from Chapter Two to look specifically at how economic concepts are related to, and usefully applied in, the effective performance of enrollment management tasks. Enrollment management has clearly become a big business within higher education, and institutional researchers are often called on to contribute to their institution's enrollment management efforts or perhaps serve as the enrollment management office. The success or failure of enrollment management efforts can have significant ramifications for an institution, particularly those that are more heavily reliant on tuition revenue to fund their operations. DesJardins and Bell describe how the economic concept of elasticity is a central part of effective enrollment management. They end with a discussion of the economics of price discrimination and how this is used in enrollment management decisions relating to financial aid offers.

In Chapter Five, Robert Toutkoushian focuses on how economic concepts can be applied to labor market issues for faculty. Institutional researchers are often called on to work with data on faculty and report them in various forms to internal and external audiences. Features of the academic labor market, such as pay differences for faculty in the finance department versus faculty in the history department, can be better understood through the application of economic concepts and models. The chapter begins with a discussion of the four types of activities that institutional researchers perform with regard to faculty. Toutkoushian then examines how economists describe the decision-making process faculty use for allocating their time between activities such as work versus other activities and teaching versus research. This discussion is followed by an explanation of the labor market for faculty and how the forces of supply and demand can affect many of the data elements that institutional researchers observe relating to faculty. The chapter concludes with a focus on the issues surrounding part-time and full-time faculty. This portion builds on work that Toutkoushian has previously conducted to examine how supply and demand factors influence the higher concentration of women among part-time faculty.

Finally, in the concluding chapter, Michael Paulsen and Robert Toutkoushian briefly review the key contributions of economics to IR in the past and the present and then provide some examples and recommendations for expanding the connections between economics and IR through new or extended uses of public sector economics in future IR applications.

Collectively, we hope that these chapters will serve as a solid introduction to economics for institutional researchers, administrators, and other higher education scholars and practitioners who are not trained economists and yet would like to know how certain key economic concepts and theories can be used to enhance their work.

Robert K. Toutkoushian
Michael B. Paulsen
Editors

ROBERT K. TOUTKOUSHIAN *is associate professor of education in the Department of Educational Leadership and Policy Studies at Indiana University.*

MICHAEL B. PAULSEN *is professor of higher education in the Department of Educational Policy and Leadership Studies at the University of Iowa.*

NEW DIRECTIONS FOR INSTITUTIONAL RESEARCH • DOI: 10.1002/ir

1

This chapter introduces the key economic concepts, models, and methods that can help inform institutional research in higher education.

Overview of Economic Concepts, Models, and Methods for Institutional Research

Michael B. Paulsen, Robert K. Toutkoushian

The discipline of economics can be traced back to the pioneering work of Adam Smith (1776). In the subsequent two hundred years, economics has blossomed into a social science that has contributed to countless fields. In this introductory chapter, we provide an overview of some of the key economic concepts, models, and methods relevant to the work of institutional research (IR) professionals. Given the size and breadth of the field, and the page constraints within which we have to accomplish this chapter's goals, our review necessarily misses many important concepts that may be helpful to institutional researchers who want to understand economics. Therefore, at the end of this chapter, we provide a list of readings that may be of interest to those who want to delve further into the subject.

Economics as a discipline is greatly misunderstood by the general public. If one were to ask the person on the street to name the first word that came to mind when hearing the word *economics,* likely responses would include *money, profit, business,* and perhaps *dull, boring,* and *difficult.* Economics has even been referred to as the dismal science by various commentators. Although many people equate economics with professional fields such as finance and accounting, it has much more in common with other social and behavioral sciences such as sociology or psychology and even with natural sciences like physics.

NEW DIRECTIONS FOR INSTITUTIONAL RESEARCH, no. 132, Winter 2006 © Wiley Periodicals, Inc.
Published online in Wiley InterScience (www.interscience.wiley.com) • DOI: 10.1002/ir.193

The field of economics is frequently broken down into two main areas of inquiry: microeconomics and macroeconomics. *Microeconomics* examines the decision-making process for smaller units within the economy. A typical microeconomics course is broken into two parts: economics of the individual and economics of organizations. *Macroeconomics* deals with problems at a more aggregate level. Macroeconomists might study how to measure the performance of a state or national economy, whereas a microeconomist would focus on how the prices for goods and services are determined and how changes in such prices affect consumer (individual) or producer (organization) behavior. Another branch of economics, known as econometrics, cuts across all of these areas of inquiry. *Econometrics* is the application of statistics to the study of economic problems. Although there are macroeconomic topics of relevance for higher education, we focus exclusively on microeconomics in this chapter. For readers interested in more detailed and in-depth explanations of the general microeconomic concepts, models, and methods presented in this chapter, we encourage them to consult some of the fine microeconomic textbooks available at the introductory level, such as Mankiw (forthcoming) or McEachern (2006), or at the intermediate level, such as Pindyck and Rubinfeld (2005) or Frank (2003).

The Economic Approach

The textbook definition of economics is that it is the study of how best to meet unlimited wants when there are not enough resources to meet them all. Some common features of economic analysis underlie every aspect of work in the field. The first is the reliance on theoretical models to describe how decision makers act in different situations (see, for example, Pindyck and Rubinfeld, 2005). Economists ask the following three questions when examining a decision-making process:

- Who are the decision makers?
- What goals are the decision makers trying to achieve?
- What constraints do the decision makers face?

Because there are not enough resources to do everything that the decision maker would like, hard choices have to be made about what can, and cannot, be done in a given situation. Therefore, the economic approach views decision makers as using an *optimization* process to maximize goals subject to resource constraints. Table 1.1 shows some examples of pursuing goals in the face of limited resources that apply to higher education settings, such as a student deciding whether to attend college, a faculty member deciding how to allocate time between teaching and research, and an enrollment manager deciding which students to admit. Economists use this fundamental approach to conceptualize, model, and analyze decision-making processes in virtually any problem or situation.

NEW DIRECTIONS FOR INSTITUTIONAL RESEARCH • DOI: 10.1002/ir

Table 1.1. Examples of Economic Problems in Higher Education

Topic	Deciding Whether to Go to College: High School Senior	Allocating Time Between Teaching and Research: Faculty Member	Deciding Which Students to Admit: Enrollment Manager
Question 1: Who are the decision makers?	High school senior and her family	Faculty member	The enrollment manager; other administrators who set general admissions policies
Question 2: What goal is the decision maker trying to achieve?	Maximize her lifetime utility	Maximize her utility	Maximize reputation net income
Question 3: What constraints does the decision maker face?	Time and income/wealth	Time	Classroom and dormitory space; income from governments and donors to offset tuition

This optimization process may be characterized graphically as the point where the decision maker's goals are consistent with the constraints. Figure 1.1 provides a general depiction of this optimization.

In this figure, a decision maker has to decide how to use two resources (A and B) to reach a goal, subject to the constraint that there are only so many units of A and B to use. At the point where the goal or objective function is tangent to the constraint line, the decision maker is maximizing the goal subject to this constraint because any other allocation of resources, aside from A* and B*, would not be as successful at achieving the goal.

Economics focuses on the way in which these decisions are made, and the emphasis on money in much of economics is a result of this approach because some organizations, such as business firms, have profit maximization as their assumed goal. The "dismal science" label perhaps reflects the emphasis on scarcity and the necessary decisions that follow from this. The labeling of economics as a difficult subject follows in part from the heavy reliance on mathematics and quantitative analysis to describe the actions of decision makers.

Economists typically make a series of *assumptions* in theoretical models about how decision makers act and the setting in which they operate. These assumptions—for example, ceteris paribus, or other things held constant—are intended to simplify the model so that attention can be focused on a particular aspect of the decision maker's problem. For example, an economist who is studying the effects of financial aid on a student's decision to attend college might make simplifying assumptions about

Figure 1.1. Depiction of Optimization in Economic Models

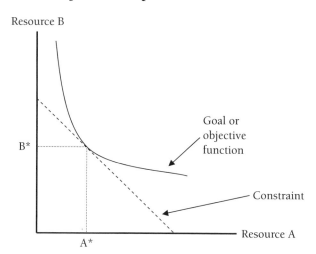

the student's sources of income, the choices available to her, and the satisfaction she receives from alternatives. These assumptions have led some to criticize economic models on the grounds that they are too unrealistic to describe the problem at hand. Without such assumptions, however, it would be very difficult, if not impossible, to examine the effects of particular factors on the behavior of individuals and organizations because the resulting model would be intractable. Furthermore, Friedman (1953) argued that the real value of a model lies not in the accuracy of its assumptions but rather in the accuracy of the predictions that are obtained from the model. Therefore, it is the capacity of economic models to predict and explain the behavior of individuals and organizations in response to changes in institutional policies or environmental factors that makes them particularly useful as analytical frameworks for institutional researchers and other data or policy analysts.

A second key feature of economic analysis is the notion of *opportunity costs* (see, for example, Frank, 2003; Paulsen, 1989). Whenever an individual or an organization makes a choice to do one thing, other alternative choices are forgone due to scarce resources. For example, when a high school graduate of traditional age decides to attend college full time and not enter the job market, that student's forgone earnings while attending college constitutes a substantial opportunity cost of college. In fact, research has shown college enrollment rates to be positively related to changes in the overall rate of unemployment (Heller, 1999; Kane, 1999). Or when a college-bound student decides to enroll at Indiana University, she gives up the option of enrolling at the University of Iowa or at other universities due to her time and income constraints. Opportunity costs, broadly defined, rep-

Figure 1.2. Production Possibilities Frontier for an Individual Faculty Member

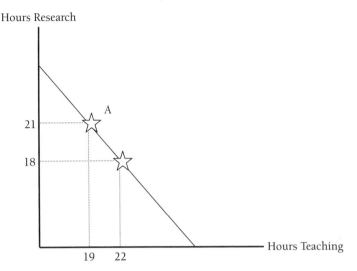

resent the value of the next-best alternative that could have been chosen by the decision maker. One way of representing opportunity costs is through a production possibilities frontier (PPF). Figure 1.2 depicts a production possibilities frontier for a faculty member who has forty hours per week to allocate between teaching and research.

Suppose that the faculty member is currently at point A, where he spends nineteen hours each week on teaching activities and twenty-one hours each week on research. If his institution adopted a new policy requiring faculty to spend at least twenty-two hours each week on teaching, this would mean giving up three hours on research. Thus, the opportunity cost to the faculty member represents the value of those three hours that can no longer be spent on research.

A third important feature of economic analysis is the emphasis on *comparative statics*, which generally refers to how an equilibrium or outcome would change if something else (typically a constraint) changes. A graphical example of comparative statics would be to determine in Figure 1.1 how the resource allocation (A^*, B^*) would change if the constraint line were to shift outward or inward, or pivot to the left or right. In fact, much of policy analysis can be thought of as actions that lead to changes in the constraints that decision makers face. A comparative statics question in higher education research might be how the faculty member's time allocation between teaching and research shown in Figure 1.2 would change if the rewards for teaching were increased. Economic tools are arguably better at examining how an equilibrium will change than they are at determining how the equilibrium was reached in the first place. For example, the economic model of student choice may be less useful at predicting which specific institutions most students attend—due to the many factors that students take into account when forming preferences and making decisions—but would be more useful at determining how student decisions might change as their financial aid, family income, or another factor changes, all else equal.

Economic Theory of Individual Behavior

The first half of almost any principles-level microeconomics course is typically dedicated to the economic theory of how individuals make decisions. Individuals are the decision makers in this context. Every one of us makes countless decisions throughout the day: what to eat, what to buy, whether to work, and so on. This also applies to higher education in many different ways. Students must make decisions about whether to go to college and, if so, which institution to attend, whether to transfer or stay at their current institution, which major to pursue, and how much time and effort to devote to their classes. Faculty members also make decisions about how to allocate their time between teaching, research, and service activities; what research projects to pursue; where to seek employment; and whether to stay at their institution or look for another job.

Economists argue that the goal for individuals is to maximize the utility or satisfaction from their actions (see Pindyck and Rubinfeld, 2005). *Utility* is a construct used to represent the satisfaction that individuals receive from the goods and services that they consume. An *indifference curve* is used to represent the various combinations of goods and services that give an individual the same level of utility. It is important to note that economists do not assign fixed values of utility to goods and services, but rather allow for people to derive different levels of satisfaction from the same good or service.

Individuals face two major constraints that inhibit the amount of utility that they can achieve. First, they need income in order to purchase goods and services. Thus, a person's income limits the amount of satisfaction that he or she can attain. Figure 1.3 shows an example for a student who wants to allocate her income between higher education (*x*-axis) and all other goods and services (*y*-axis). She has a fixed amount of income ($50,000) to allocate between higher education and all other goods. She also knows that she would receive utility from going to college and from buying other goods and services, and the utility from possible combinations of college and other goods are represented by the indifference curves. Given her budget constraint, the highest utility she can attain is 300 utils (U = 300). Although she would prefer any combination along the indifference curve labeled "U = 400," this is not possible given her income constraint. Therefore, point A constitutes this consumer's equilibrium, where her utility has been max-

Figure 1.3. Student Choice Regarding College Attendance

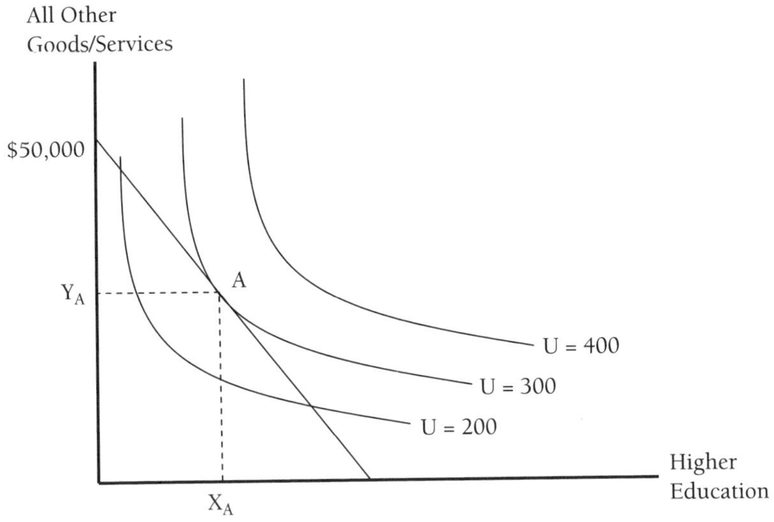

imized, given her budget constraint, by optimally allocating her resources—that is, by dividing her budget between X_A units of higher education and Y_A units of other goods and services.

This economic model of individual decision making can also be used for a variety of analyses of consumer (student) behavior, using the method of comparative statics—comparing two states of equilibrium where an outcome differs because a parameter, such as a constraint faced by a decision maker, changes. For example, Figure 1.4 reconsiders the optimization process by which the student consumer portrayed in Figure 1.3 seeks to maximize her utility, given her budget constraint, by allocating her resources between units of higher education and other goods and services. Each of the colleges in the student's choice set informs her that they are offering her a $1,000 tuition discount. This reduces the price of college for this student, and Figure 1.4 represents the lower price of higher education by rotating the student's initial budget constraint so that its intercept on the horizontal axis is farther from the origin. The new equilibrium is at point B, where the student once again optimally allocates her resources and achieves a higher level of utility (U = 400) with her new budget constraint, by allocating her resources between X_B units of higher education and Y_B other goods and services.

Another central feature of the economic theory of how individuals make decisions is the economist's assumption of *rational behavior* on the part of decision makers (DesJardins and Toutkoushian, 2005. Although this assumption is very important for understanding the economic model

Figure 1.4. A Tuition Discount and Student Choice Regarding College Attendance

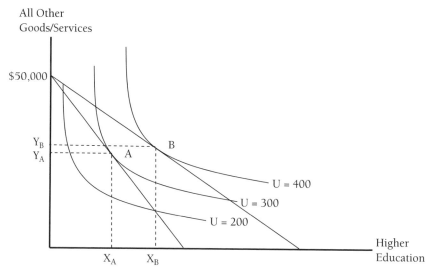

of decision-making behavior, the economist's conceptualization of rational behavior is often misunderstood and misused by social scientists—including some economists—and policy analysts. The economic concept of rational behavior assumes that the individual decision maker seeks to maximize his or her own utility subject to the limitations posed by his or her budget constraint. However, it is important to understand the meaning of this assumption in terms of the basic elements that, in combination, constitute the essence of the model of optimal decision making. First, the map of indifference curves represents the *preferences* of an individual decision maker and the utility or perceived values he or she assigns to each possible combination of goods and services. But a consumer's preferences for any particular combination of goods and services—and the perceived values and utilities the consumer assigns to it—are unique, subjective, and idiosyncratic. These preferences can vary considerably from one individual to another because of individual differences in factors that may influence one's preferences. For example, the formation of preferences may reflect individual differences in early home, school, and community environments; religious, moral, and ideological views; or access to relevant and accurate information or experiences with respect to each combination of goods and services. As a result, two individuals with the same budget constraint could make different choices about allocating their incomes between units of higher education and other goods and services; yet both would be behaving rationally if each acts to maximize his or her own util-

New Directions for Institutional Research • DOI: 10.1002/ir

ity or satisfaction, based on his or her own unique and different preferences, subject to the budget constraints each faces.

The second element in the model of optimal decision making is the set of *constraints*, particularly income or time constraints, that a decision maker faces, which represent the decision maker's resources or opportunities for use in the pursuit of higher levels of utility or satisfaction. Consumers clearly differ in the constraints they face in their decision making, particularly in terms of income constraints. As a result, two individuals with the same preferences for combinations of higher education and other goods and services but different budget constraints could make different choices about college attendance, yet both would be behaving rationally.

The economist's framework for analyzing individual decision making, including its assumption of rational behavior, can also be used to look at how individuals allocate another important resource, their time, between competing activities such as work and leisure. The constraint in this model is not income but rather "time," because individuals only have so many hours per day and days per year to divide among activities. The individual's objective or goal is to maximize utility from how he or she spends time. According to this model, people derive utility from both the work that they do and the goods and services that they can buy with the income that they earn from working. People also obtain utility from not working because they can spend their time doing other things that give them pleasure; however, time spent in leisure has an opportunity cost because it takes time away from working, thus lowering income. Figure 1.5 depicts this situation for a faculty member who has to allocate discretionary time per day between doing faculty work and all other activities. The *x*-axis measures hours per day spent in nonwork activities, and the *y*-axis represents the income earned from working.

Figure 1.5. Depiction of Faculty Time Allocation

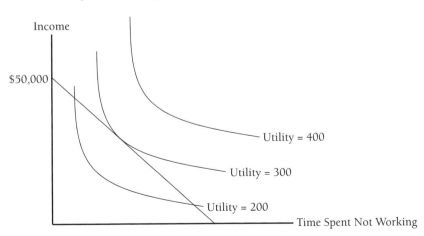

Another central element of economic analysis is based on the concept of *marginalism* and the method of *marginal analysis* (Frank, 2003; Paulsen, 1989; Pindyck and Rubinfeld, 2005). Marginal analysis provides another way of representing and thinking about the economic model of optimal decision making. Economists emphasize decisions made "at the margin." Examples of such decisions would include a current college student deciding whether to invest in an additional year of college, a faculty member deciding whether to engage in an additional research project, or a college's office of admissions deciding whether to enroll an additional high-ability, high-income student with merit aid. In these cases, the term *marginal* is a synonym for *additional,* and the pursuit of the marginal year of college, the marginal research project, and the marginal student enrolled would yield marginal benefits (MB) and marginal costs (MC) for the decision maker.

The MB-MC analytical framework is highly generalizable and applicable to the analysis of optimal decision-making processes in many situations. The only element of the model that changes across situations is the nature of the marginal benefits or marginal costs that the decision maker considers. For example, what constitutes a marginal benefit or a marginal cost would vary across the three scenarios already introduced: a student considering investing in an additional year of college, a faculty member considering engaging in an additional research project, and an enrollment manager considering enrolling more high-ability students with merit aid. For the student, the MB of investing in an additional year of college would be the student's perception of the marginal rate of return to college, and the MC would be the marginal interest costs of funds required to invest in another year of college (see, for example, Paulsen, 2001a). For the faculty member, MB could include additional compensation for publications, greater compensation, status and job security due to earning tenure, and the like. MC could include opportunities forgone due to less time spent on teaching, such as loss of income for teaching a summer course or an extra section of a regular semester course, and less positive student evaluations due to less time for improvement of teaching. Finally, for the enrollment manager, MB might include additional tuition and fee revenue and less tangible benefits such as a student's contributions to the institution's reputation, the quality of its educational experiences, or the diversity of its student body. MC would include the expense of merit aid and the additional instructional, technological, and other educational costs incurred.

Figure 1.6 illustrates optimal decision making using marginal analysis. As long as the MB of an additional unit of college, research, or student enrollment exceeds its MC, it is worthwhile to pursue or acquire additional units. In Figure 1.6, for any quantity of units below Q_B, such as Q_A, the MB from the last unit (\$3) exceeds its MC (\$1), indicating that Q_A units represent a less than optimal quantity. However, if the MC of an additional unit exceeds its MB, then the decision maker would be better off by reducing the number of units acquired. In Figure 1.6, for any quantity of units above Q_B, such as Q_C, the MC from the last unit (\$3) exceeds its MB (\$1), indicating

Figure 1.6. Optimal Decision Making Using Marginal Analysis

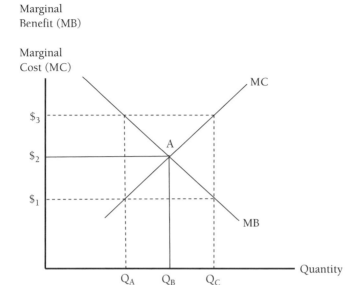

that Q_C units represent an amount greater than the optimal quantity. The decision maker reaches the optimal number of units of college, research, or student enrollment only when the last unit acquired yields marginal benefits equal to marginal costs (MB = MC). The optimal quantity is represented in Figure 1.6 by Q_B, which corresponds to point A where MB = MC—that is, MB = $2 *and* MC = $2.

Economic Theory of Markets

In capitalistic societies, most goods and services are bought and sold in markets. Markets can vary greatly in size and scope and are used to determine the price charged for goods and services and how they should be allocated among potential buyers. The *economic theory of competitive markets* holds that these decisions are made based on the intersection of the market *supply and demand* curves, as shown in Figure 1.7 (Mankiw, forthcoming; Pindyck and Rubinfeld, 2005). These supply and demand curves come from the decisions made by individuals and organizations as described earlier. The *individual's demand curve* for higher education, for example, is obtained by varying the price of higher education and observing the new amounts of higher education that she would consume at each price. By changing the wage rate and observing the new amounts of hours worked, one can obtain an individual's labor supply curve.

Figure 1.7. Equilibrium in Competitive Markets

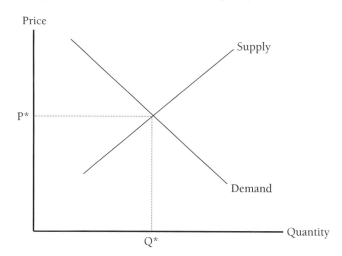

The *market demand curve* is the sum of all of the demand curves for individuals that arise from the decisions individuals make. The downward slope indicates that as the price of the good decreases, individuals would be willing and able to purchase more of the good. Similarly, the *market supply curve* is the sum of the supply curves for all suppliers of the good or service. As the price rises, the quantity supplied would also rise, leading to an upward sloping market supply curve.

The *equilibrium price* in a market is found where the *quantity demanded* equals the *quantity supplied.* If prices were set above this level, then quantity supplied would exceed quantity demanded and suppliers would have an incentive to reduce prices. And when prices are below equilibrium, quantity demanded would exceed quantity supplied; buyers would increase their offers and, as a result, drive up market prices. Because various forces lead to shifts in the market demand and supply curves, equilibrium can be thought of as a continuously moving target toward which the market is always being drawn.

Figure 1.8 illustrates one of the many applications of the economic theory of markets that can be very useful for institutional researchers and other policy analysts: how students with different characteristics can have very different degrees of responsiveness to changes in price—in other words, tuition in higher education settings (Paulsen, 1998). Economists use the concept of elasticity in two ways to describe the sensitivity of demand to changes in price. The first way is to calculate the elasticity at any point along the demand curve (point elasticity), which is discussed in Chapter Four of this volume. The second way is to describe the overall steepness of the demand curve as being either relatively high in its elasticity (flat or nearly flat) or relatively low in its elasticity (steep).

Figure 1.8. Demand, Supply, and Variations in Price Elasticity

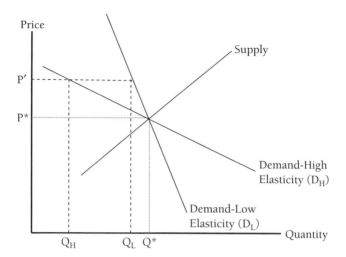

Figure 1.8 presents one upward-sloping supply curve and two down-ward-sloping demand curves. One demand curve portrays students who demonstrate relatively high elasticity (D_H) in response to changes in the price of college—that is, tuition. The other demand curve portrays students who show relatively low elasticity (D_L) in response to changes in tuition. Research has consistently shown that, just like consumers in other markets, students from lower-income backgrounds are highly elastic in their responsiveness to tuition increases, while their higher-income counterparts show relatively low elasticity (Heller, 1997). In the figure, the differences between high and low tuition elasticities are illustrated in the notable differences in the steepness of the two demand curves and in the decreases in the quantity of students enrolled (Q) that accompany increases in the price of college (P). In particular, as the price of college increases from P^* to P', the quantity of enrollment among high-elastic, lower-income students decreases by the amount $Q^* - Q_H$, which is substantially greater than a corresponding decrease for low-elastic, higher-income students by the amount $Q^* - Q_L$. Finally, the elasticity construct is generalizable to applications assessing students' enrollment responses to other changes in price-related variables besides just tuition, such as changes in student fees, institutional aid, state or federal grants, federal or private loans, and other price subsidies such as private scholarships.

Economists recognize, however, that for many reasons, higher education is a unique service that does not fit perfectly into the competitive market model. First, the model is premised on the assumption that the goal of the suppliers is profit maximization. It is generally understood that most institutions of higher education do not act to maximize profits; however, economists have offered a number of alternative goals, including revenue maximization, cost minimization, maximization of discretionary income, and reputation (Bowen, 1980; Garvin, 1980; Paulsen, 2000).

A second important feature of higher education is that there are *positive externalities* associated with its consumption (Baum and Payea, 2004; Fatima and Paulsen, 2004; Paulsen, 2001b). This means that when individual students invest in higher education, not only do they benefit directly in the form of private benefits such as higher lifetime earnings, but others in society also benefit from their higher education. These benefits to society, which are often called *external benefits* or *externalities*, include monetary and nonmonetary benefits, and the latter can be particularly difficult to quantify; however, because of their existence, a competitive market would produce too little higher education from society's point of view. This underinvestment occurs because individual students who are investing in higher education cannot capture or internalize these benefits to society. Indeed, such benefits are literally external to the investment decision of any individual student. The individual student's *willingness to pay* for higher education is based on his or her perceptions of the value of the private or internal benefits he or she will acquire. However, society has a willingness to pay for the external benefits that accrue to it.

To remedy this problem of underinvestment in and underproduction of higher education in the presence of positive externalities, a number of entities, including governments and individuals, subsidize some of the costs of higher education. In the public sector, the primary source of such subsidies takes the form of state appropriations to institutions, whereas the primary source of such subsidies for institutions in the private sector arises from fundraising and endowment income. Growth in these subsidies slows the growth of tuition, which stimulates greater enrollment.

Because of the important role of subsidies in the higher education enterprise, Gordon Winston (1997) argues that higher education prices are set according to the following formula: Price = Cost − subsidy. In contrast, the equation Price = Cost + profit is often used to describe price setting in much of the for-profit world. Virtually all institutions use subsidies from one source or another to reduce the price charged to students. Toutkoushian (2001) showed, for example, that in 1995, state, national, and local governments covered approximately 72 percent of the net price of public higher education. Although private institutions are rarely subsidized by governments, they also receive significant revenues from private sources as well as sponsored research grants that also help to lower the net price charged to students by about 37 percent in 1995.

Winston's pricing equation for institutions of higher education is also helpful for understanding the causes of trends in higher education pricing. This illustrates that price increases could be due to rising costs, falling subsidies, or some combination of the two. This point is often lost on policy-

Figure 1.9. Increasing Costs and Rising Tuition

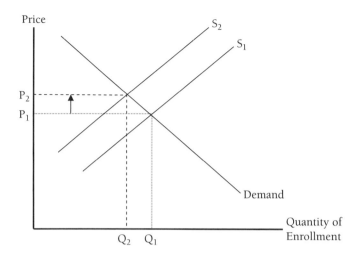

makers and even the general public, who have observed a long history of tuition increases that exceed the rate of inflation. In the competitive market model, cost increases are the primary cause of rising prices. The history for the United States, in fact, shows that state funding for higher education has fallen as a share of total revenue, dropping from 57 percent in 1975 to 47 percent in 1995 (Toutkoushian, 2001). As Figure 1.9 shows, for public institutions in particular, increasing costs—such as administrative, student services or instructional costs, ceteris paribus—that are not offset by commensurate increases in state appropriations would lead to an upward shift in market supply, and for a given demand, would lead to higher prices—in other words, tuition inflation.

Economic Theory of Organizational Behavior

The economist's model of how organizations such as colleges behave is also instructive for understanding many aspects of higher education. Economists think of colleges in much the same way as other organizations in that they rely on an input-production-output to deliver higher education services. In this model, organizations take a series of inputs, run them through a production process, and create outputs from the inputs (see, for example, Frank 2003). The outputs are then used to achieve particular goals and objectives for the organization. This model is most often used to describe for-profit firms that produce goods such as automobiles and books. The inputs are the raw materials that are converted into products. The production process represents the plant, equipment, workers, and technology used to make products. The outputs then represent the final goods or products produced by the firm. In this instance, the goal of the firm is clear: maximize profits.

Does this description hold for institutions of higher education? There are a number of reasons that this model would hold at some level of abstraction for higher education (Hopkins, 1990). Both students and faculty can be thought of as inputs that colleges and universities use to produce teaching and research outputs. The classrooms, facilities, faculty, curriculum, and others are part of the production process institutions use for educational purposes. The knowledge gained by students; the articles, books, and patents derived from research activities; and the services provided to governments and other entities can all be considered outputs. This general framework can be applied to nonprofit as well as for-profit institutions.

Nevertheless, the production model in higher education is more complex than in other sectors of the economy in some important ways (Rothschild and White, 1995). First, students are both an input and part of the production process, in that they have to exert effort to learn. Similarly, faculty are an input for producing research and also constitute part of the production process for producing teaching. Second, postsecondary institutions produce multiple outputs in the areas of teaching, research, and service. Many policymakers fail to recognize this when they calculate statistics such as expenditures per student because some of these costs are incurred to produce research and service outputs. Third, institutions are constrained in their ability to acquire better inputs. If Ford or GM wanted to build better automobiles, they could easily go out and acquire better raw materials such as steel and glass (albeit at a higher price) to accomplish this goal. In contrast, institutions of higher education can use as inputs only the subset of students who apply to their institution, are admitted, and accept their offer. Economists would say that institutions are constrained by students' demand for the institution. Similarly, institutions are constrained by faculty members' demand and supply curves in their ability to acquire better faculty for producing research and teaching outputs. Finally, the production analogy is complicated by the fact that the goals of postsecondary institutions are sometimes ambiguous and difficult to measure. As we noted, most economists agree that institutions of higher education do not attempt to maximize profits, although some have suggested related goals such as maximizing revenue or maximizing the institution's discretionary budget (Bowen, 1980; Paulsen, 2000). However, while other possible and probable goals, such as maximizing student learning and gains to society through research, are noble, they are also next to impossible to measure. Without such measures, it becomes difficult to examine the activities of institutions and determine without considerable ambiguity and imprecision how they contribute to these goals.

Recommended Readings

We hope that this chapter has helped provide some insight into how economists view the world and, in particular, how they approach problems facing higher education. For those who are interested in learning more about economic reasoning, we recommend a number of readings.

General Background. These readings explain in greater detail the general models and approaches that economists use. Excellent overviews of economic reasoning can be found in Hausman (1989), Hirshleifer (1985), and Aaron (1994). Among the countless introductory-level textbooks on microeconomics that have been published, two of the more successful and interesting of these are Mankiw (2006) and McEachern (2006). At the intermediate level, the textbooks rely more heavily on mathematics to explain key concepts. The textbook by Pindyck and Rubinfeld (2005) is among the more accessible in this group. Finally, for readers interested in the economics of labor markets, we recommend the textbook by Ehrenberg and Smith (2000).

Economics and Education. Relatively few books have focused on the application of economics to education. Among the exceptions are the early work by Blaug (1970), Thurow (1970), and Perlman (1973); the somewhat later work by Garvin (1980), Cohn and Geske (1990), Hoenack and Collins (1990), and Johnes (1993); and more recently, the books by Belfield (2000), and Paulsen and Smart (2001). In addition, Ehrenberg (2004) published an informative overview of the types of econometric studies that have been focused on higher education. It is more common for economists to focus on particular aspects of higher education in their work. For example, Hoxby (2004) edited an excellent volume on the economist's view of how students make decisions about their postsecondary education. Toutkoushian (2003a) reviewed how economic models can be used to examine trends in the labor market for postsecondary faculty and looked at the economic approach to pay equity studies in higher education (2002, 2003b).

Historical Works. Many works in the field of economics have had particular significance for higher education. Here, we highlight a few of these. Schultz (1961, 1963), Becker (1964), and Mincer (1974) were among the first economists to describe the notion of human capital and how higher education is a means for individuals to acquire it. This work became the basis for much of the subsequent research conducted by economists and others on topics such as the investment in human capital, college choice, and the return on education. In addition, some economists have argued that colleges act as an efficient screening mechanism for employers (Spence, 1973; Stiglitz, 1975). This has spurred a debate that continues to this day as to whether colleges primarily sort students based on ability or impart knowledge and skills that become part of their human capital, or some combination of the two. Becker's article on the theory of time allocation (1965) emphasized that time is a scarce resource to be allocated in much the same way as income or wealth, thereby expanding economic reasoning to situations outside of product markets.

Readings on Economics for the Layperson. Several books and articles offer a more accessible and sometimes lighthearted look at economics. Perhaps the best known of these is the recent best-seller *Freakonomics,* by Levitt and Dubner (2005). The authors use economic reasoning to look at a wide range of topics, including the connection between sumo wrestlers and teachers. Although she was not an economist (and would have probably objected to being labeled as one), Ayn Rand used her novels such as *Atlas Shrugged* (1957) to describe key economic concepts such as rationality, the pursuit of self-interest, and the private and social benefits of capitalism and competitive, free markets. Finally, Roger Arnold's recent book (2005) offers numerous illustrations of how economists think, each embedded in one or more "economic stories" on topics ranging from drug busts to SUVs to playing tennis.

References

Aaron, H. "Distinguished Lecture on Economics in Government: Public Policy, Values, and Consciousness." *Journal of Economic Perspectives,* 1994, *8*(2), 3–21.

Arnold, R. *How to Think Like an Economist.* Mason, Ohio: Thompson/Southwestern, 2005.

Baum, S., and Payea, K. *Education Pays: The Benefits of Higher Education for Individuals and Society.* New York: College Board, 2004.

Becker, G. *Human Capital: A Theoretical and Empirical Analysis with Special Reference to Education.* Cambridge, Mass.: National Bureau of Economic Research, 1964.

Becker, G. "A Theory of the Allocation of Time." *Economic Journal,* 1965, *75*(299), 493–517.

Belfield, C. *Economic Principles for Education: Theory and Evidence.* Northampton, Mass.: Edward Elgar, 2000.

Blaug, M. *An Introduction to the Economics of Education.* London: Penguin Press, 1970.

Bowen, H. *The Costs of Higher Education: How Much Do Colleges and Universities Spend per Student and How Much Should They Spend?* San Francisco: Jossey-Bass, 1980.

Cohn, E., and Geske, T. *The Economics of Education.* (3rd ed.) Pergamon Press, 1990.

DesJardins, S., and Toutkoushian, R. "Are Students Really Rational? The Development of Rational Thought and Its Application to Student Choice." In J. Smart (ed.), *Higher Education: Handbook of Theory and Research.* New York: Springer, 2005.

Ehrenberg, R. "Econometric Studies of Higher Education." *Journal of Econometrics,* 2004, *121*(1–2), 19–37.

Ehrenberg, R., and Smith, R. *Modern Labor Economics: Theory and Public Policy.* (7th ed.) Reading, Mass.: Addison-Wesley, 2000.

Fatima, N., and Paulsen, M. "Higher Education and State Workforce Productivity in the 1990s." *Thought and Action: The NEA Higher Education Journal,* 2004, *20*(1), 75–94.

Frank, R. *Microeconomics and Behavior.* (5th ed.) New York: McGraw-Hill, 2003.

Friedman, M. (ed.). *Essays in Positive Economics.* Chicago: University of Chicago Press, 1953.

Garvin, D. *The Economics of University Behavior.* New York: Academic Press, 1980.

Hausman, D. "Economic Methodology in a Nutshell." *Journal of Economic Perspectives,* 1989, *3*(2), 115–127.

Heller, D. "Student Price Response in Higher Education: An Update to Leslie and Brinkman." *Journal of Higher Education*, 1997, *68*(6), 624–659.

Heller, D. "The Effects of Tuition and State Financial Aid on Public College Enrollment." *Review of Higher Education*, 1999, *23*(1), 65–89.

Hirshleifer, J. "The Expanding Domain of Economics." *American Economic Review*, 1985, *75*(6), 53–68.

Hoenack, S., and Collins, E. (eds.). *The Economics of American Universities.* Albany: State University of New York Press, 1990.

Hopkins, S. "The Higher Education Production Function: Theoretical Foundations and Empirical Findings." In S. Hoenack and E. Collins (eds.), *The Economics of American Universities.* Albany: State University of New York Press, 1990.

Hoxby, C. (ed.). *College Choices: The Economics of Where to Go, When to Go, and How to Pay for It.* Cambridge, Mass.: National Bureau of Economic Research, 2004.

Johnes, G. *The Economics of Education.* New York: St. Martin's Press, 1993.

Kane, T. *The Price of Admission.* Washington, D.C.: Brookings Institution, 1999.

Levitt, S., and Dubner, S. *Freakonomics: A Rogue Economist Explores the Hidden Side of Everything.* New York: HarperCollins, 2005.

Mankiw, G. *Principles of Microeconomics.* (4th ed.) Cincinnati, Ohio: South-Western Publishing, 2006.

McEachern, W. *Microeconomics: A Contemporary Introduction.* (7th ed.) Cincinnati, Ohio: South-Western Publishing, 2006.

Mincer, J. *Schooling, Experience, and Earnings.* Cambridge, Mass.: National Bureau of Economic Research, 1974.

Paulsen, M. "Ten Essential Economic Concepts Every Administrator Should Know." *Journal for Higher Education Management,* 1989, *5*(1), 9–17.

Paulsen, M. "Recent Research on the Economics of Attending College: Returns on Investment and Responsiveness to Price." *Research in Higher Education,* 1998, *39*(4), 471–489.

Paulsen, M. "Economic Perspectives on Rising College Tuition: A Theoretical and Empirical Exploration." In J. Smart (ed.), *Higher Education: Handbook of Theory and Research.* New York: Agathon Press, 2000.

Paulsen, M. "The Economics of Human Capital and Investment in Higher Education." In M. Paulsen and J. Smart (eds.), *The Finance of Higher Education: Theory, Research, Policy and Practice.* New York: Agathon Press, 2001a.

Paulsen, M. "The Economics of the Public Sector: The Nature and Role of Public Policy in the Finance of Higher Education." In M. Paulsen and J. Smart (eds.), *The Finance of Higher Education: Theory, Research, Policy and Practice.* New York: Agathon Press, 2001b.

Paulsen, M., and Smart, J. (eds.). *The Finance of Higher Education: Theory, Research, Policy and Practice.* New York: Agathon Press, 2001.

Perlman, R. *The Economics of Education: Conceptual Problems and Policy Issues.* New York: McGraw-Hill, 1973.

Pindyck, R., and Rubinfeld, D. *Microeconomics.* (6th ed.) Upper Saddle River, N.J.: Prentice Hall, 2005.

Rand, A. *Atlas Shrugged.* New York: Plume, 1999. (Originally published 1957.)

Rothschild, M., and White, L. "The Analytics of Pricing in Higher Education and Other Services in Which Customers Are Inputs." *Journal of Political Economy,* 1995, *103*, 573–586.

Schultz, T. "Investment in Human Capital." *American Economic Review,* 1961, *51*(1), 1–17.

Schultz, T. *The Economic Value of Education.* New York: Columbia University Press, 1963.

Smith, A. *The Wealth of Nations.* New York: Barnes & Noble, 2004. (Originally published 1776.)

Spence, M. "Job Market Signaling." *Quarterly Journal of Economics,* 1973, *87*, 355–374.

Stiglitz, J. "The Theory of 'Screening,' Education, and the Distribution of Income." *American Economic Review,* 1975, *65*(3), 283–300.

Thurow, L. *Investment in Human Capital.* Belmont, Calif.: Wadsworth, 1970.

Toutkoushian, R. "Trends in Revenues and Expenditures for Public and Private Higher Education." In M. Paulsen and J. Smart (eds.), *The Finance of Higher Education: Theory, Research, Policy and Practice.* New York: Agathon Press, 2001.

Toutkoushian, R. (ed.). *Conducting Salary-Equity Studies: Alternative Approaches to Research.* New Directions for Institutional Research, no. 115. San Francisco: Jossey-Bass, 2002.

Toutkoushian, R. "What Can Labor Economics Tell Us About the Earnings and Employment Prospects for Faculty?" In J. Smart (ed.), *Higher Education: Handbook of Theory and Research.* New York: Agathon Press, 2003a.

Toutkoushian, R. (ed.). *Unresolved Issues in Conducting Salary-Equity Studies.* New Directions for Institutional Research, no. 117. San Francisco: Jossey-Bass, 2003b.

Winston, G. "Why Can't a College Be More Like a Firm?" *Change,* Sept.–Oct. 1997, pp. 33–38.

MICHAEL B. PAULSEN *is professor of higher education in the Department of Educational Policy and Leadership Studies at the University of Iowa.*

ROBERT K. TOUTKOUSHIAN *is associate professor of education in the Department of Educational Leadership and Policy Studies at Indiana University.*

NEW DIRECTIONS FOR INSTITUTIONAL RESEARCH • DOI: 10.1002/ir

2

To properly evaluate the financial contributions of each revenue source, institutional researchers must use key economic concepts in their work.

Applying Economics to Institutional Research on Higher Education Revenues

John J. Cheslock

Economists often model colleges and universities as seeking to maximize certain objectives given a set of financial constraints. Within this framework, revenues are simply the constraint that prevents the institution from marking further strides toward educational excellence, prestige, and influence. This reality led Howard Bowen (1980) to state that higher education institutions raise all the money they can. But this statement seems to clash with the environment within which many institutional researchers work, one where revenue considerations seem to be growing in importance. If higher education institutions are always raising all the money they can, how can revenue considerations become more important?

One possible explanation for this paradox is the variety of new opportunities for higher education institutions to generate dollars. Passage of the Bayh-Dole Act in 1980, which eased schools' ability to own and license patents; the growing importance of scientific knowledge in the marketplace due to advances in biotechnology and information technology; and the increased demand for adult education in response to rapidly changing skill requirements in the workplace changed the revenue landscape for colleges and universities (Bok, 2003; Slaughter and Rhoades, 2004).

An additional explanation simply disputes Bowen's description of colleges and universities. Higher education institutions may not always maximize revenues, but may instead increase revenues as needed to meet their

NEW DIRECTIONS FOR INSTITUTIONAL RESEARCH, no. 132, Winter 2006   © Wiley Periodicals, Inc.
Published online in Wiley InterScience (www.interscience.wiley.com) • DOI: 10.1002/ir.194

expected costs. With costs rising at faster rates than some traditional revenue sources, many schools must find new revenues to meet this shortfall.

Given such an environment, college and university leaders will increasingly turn to institutional researchers for insightful analyses of the financial situation of their institutions. Because the complexity of most higher education institutions makes such an examination difficult, institutional researchers need to ground their work in basic economic theory to ensure clarity. This chapter provides an introduction to the necessary theory.

General Revenue Considerations

This section presents basic concepts that economists use to describe the financial situation of an institution of higher education. These ideas help to highlight the contribution of each unit or activity to the institution's overall financial picture.

Net Revenues, Fixed Revenues, Subsidies, and Mission. To evaluate the financial impact of any activity on campus, the researcher should measure not simply the revenue generated by the activity but the net revenue generated. Net revenue equals the revenue minus the cost of the activity. Although this economic concept seems to be the obvious criterion to employ, decision makers within higher education institutions have not always used it. As I discuss later in this chapter, the use of net tuition revenue as the primary measure of relevance for tuition dollars has only recently emerged. In addition, the current discourse regarding the potential financial contributions of a variety of new entrepreneurial activities focuses more on revenue potential than the associated costs.

To place the net revenue of a specific activity within the broader financial picture of the institution, the basic utility maximization model that economists use to describe college and university behavior is helpful. James (1978) and James and Neuberger (1981) presented an influential early version of this model, which has since been extended in several directions. The organization seeks to maximize a utility function $U[Q_i, (Q_i/C_i)]$ subject to the zero-profit constraint $\Sigma C_i - \Sigma P_i Q_i - FR = 0$. Here, Q_i represents the amount produced of activity i, C_i represents the cost of producing that amount of activity i, P_i represents the revenue generated from each unit of activity i, and FR represents the amount of fixed revenue enjoyed by the institution. The last term represents revenues that are not generated from any specific activity, such as donations or income from endowment.

Within this model, each activity i produces net revenue equal to $P_i Q_i - C_i$. Activities with positive net revenue are generating profits that can help subsidize other activities. Activities with negative net revenue can continue to function because they enjoy subsidies from profit-generating activities and fixed revenues.

Using this framework, one can demonstrate several important insights regarding revenues. Consider first the fixed revenue portion of the equation.

NEW DIRECTIONS FOR INSTITUTIONAL RESEARCH • DOI: 10.1002/ir

These revenues are vital to the institution because they allow it to engage in activities that are not covering their costs. In other words, substantial fixed revenue allows a school to pursue activities that are vital to its mission but do not generate substantial amounts of revenue (Cantor and Courant, 2003).

The absence of substantial fixed revenue can make it difficult for an institution to completely fulfill its mission. In this situation, a school must identify profit-generating activities that produce enough net revenue to subsidize activities that are running deficits (Zemsky, Wegner, and Massy, 2005). These activities are not required to be a central part of the institution's mission; their role is simply to provide funding for mission-central activities (Zemsky, Wegner, and Massy, 2005). But many institutions may not have sufficient market power to generate substantial profits. Furthermore, many for-profit schools are increasingly identifying and engaging in activities that do generate profits, which reduce the available dollars for nonprofit institutions. These points highlight why substantial fixed revenue is such a valuable commodity.

An institutional researcher can use this theoretical framework to illuminate the economic situation of his or her institution. For example, activities that generate positive net revenue can be identified. Higher education institutions are increasingly engaging in a new set of activities that are primarily justified as a mechanism to improve the institution's financial situation. But little evidence exists on the extent to which these new activities actually help subsidize other activities. In all likelihood, many are not as advertised.

An institutional researcher can also describe the distribution of the institution's discretionary funds across various activities. These resources, which contain fixed revenues as well as the net revenues generated from profitable activities, are extremely important because they are the mechanism by which institutions engage in mission-central activities that do not sufficiently generate revenue. A firm understanding of their current distribution across activities is required to ensure their wise use.

A seasoned institutional researcher will quickly realize that this theoretical discussion can be quite difficult to apply in practice. Associating revenues and costs with a particular activity is greatly complicated by the joint production that occurs within colleges and universities. This complication is much greater on the cost side of the equation and consequently is well beyond the scope of this chapter. Nevertheless, these obstacles must be overcome for any serious analysis of the financial contributions of various activities to be performed.

The designation of revenues as fixed or associated with a specific activity can also present a challenge. State appropriations provide a good example. Because the financial implications of enrollment growth vary substantially across different designations, the correct assignment of state appropriations is quite important. In some cases, the assignment will be straightforward: state appropriations that are distributed purely on an enrollment-based formula would be assigned to those activities supporting enrolled students, while state appropriations that more closely resemble block grants would be fixed revenue. But in many cases, the distribution of state funds is a combination of these two extremes, and the application of this theoretical framework consequently requires thoughtful and careful analysis. These complexities are not problems inherent in the theoretical framework but simply a characteristic of the economic context of higher education that must be recognized in any rigorous examination.

Marginal Revenues. Economists regularly exhort people to think at the margin. Such an activity requires knowledge of the concepts of marginal revenue and marginal cost. Marginal revenue is the change in the total revenue from producing an additional unit of an activity, and marginal costs, which are discussed in great detail in Chapter Three, are the corresponding change in total costs.

What does it mean to think at the margin? Consider a college leader deciding whether to expand an activity on campus. If the decision were made for purely financial reasons, the expansion should take place only if the marginal revenue exceeds the marginal cost (that is, the net marginal revenue is positive). If the expansion does take place, then the increase in resources available to other activities would equal the marginal revenue minus the marginal cost.

Hence, thinking at the margin allows one to understand the financial implications of expanding or contracting certain activities. In combination with all nonfinancial considerations, this framework can help sharpen one's thinking. Zemsky, Wegner, and Massy (2005) suggest that this framework can be extended so that it is the sole criterion used to make decisions. One would need to calculate the marginal mission attainment, which is the increase in mission attainment (valued in dollars) from expanding the activity by one unit. In this case, an institution would expand an activity only if the marginal revenue plus the marginal mission attainment exceeds the marginal cost.

Thinking at the margin requires estimating the marginal revenue generated by the expansion of the activity, not an easy task. Institutional researchers will be tempted to simply assume that the marginal revenue for an expansion of one unit will equal the average revenue observed in the past. But such an assumption may be problematic.

Let us return to basic microeconomic theory to examine this issue further. For the standard model of a for-profit firm, marginal revenue equals average revenue when the firm participates in a perfectly competitive market, and marginal revenue is less than average revenue when the firm has some market power. A perfectly competitive market has many buyers and sellers, and the goods offered by the various sellers are largely the same. In most cases, firms can freely enter or exit the market (Mankiw, 2001). Within this environment, competitive pressures force each firm to simply charge the price set in the market, regardless of the amount any individual firm produces. In economics jargon, the firms are price takers.

But the markets within which higher education institutions participate are usually not perfectly competitive. Consider the market for students.

Many students are considering schools only in a relatively limited geographical range, so there are relatively few buyers. Furthermore, the education offered by the schools in their region usually differs across several important dimensions, and entry and exit are relatively rare occurrences in higher education.

Consequently, most higher education institutions are not price takers and instead have some market power. The price they can charge falls with the amount they produce because the price must be lowered in order to find new buyers for the additional output. This falling price causes the marginal revenue to be less than the average revenue.

For two reasons, however, this basic model is not always applicable to higher education. First, the model describes competition among for-profit firms, not nonprofit institutions of higher education. For activities central to their mission, colleges and universities may not be charging the full amount that the market will bear. Consequently, they often may be able to increase output without lowering their price. In this case, marginal revenue would not be less than average revenue.

Second, for many activities within higher education, the outputs are not easily measurable or not measurable at all. Hence, institutional researchers will find themselves examining the potential implications of a set increase in inputs rather than outputs. For example, the expansion of an academic department would not be in units of research, teaching, and service but instead in the number of faculty lines. And the relevant consideration for the expansion of the development office would not be in the number of fundraising appeals but instead in the number of full-time-equivalent personnel.

If the unit of analysis is an input, the marginal revenue will equal average revenue only if an additional unit of input generates the same revenue as earlier units. But the marginal returns to an input could instead be increasing or decreasing with size. For the case of development, each additional fundraiser likely produces fewer and fewer dollars, because the most promising donors are likely approached first. Hence, marginal returns are decreasing, and the marginal revenue of an additional fundraiser would be less than the average revenue produced by the existing personnel. Increasing returns are likely less common, but can occur when an activity or unit becomes more productive with size. For example, a research unit may need to reach a critical mass of faculty members or lab space before the institution can secure large grants in that area.

The discussion in this section clearly suggests that marginal revenue often does not equal average revenue. But institutional researchers will be tempted to use average revenue in their analysis because an estimate of marginal revenue requires a great deal of knowledge about the area of the institution under question. And even with such knowledge, tremendous uncertainty exists. But an uncertain and imperfect calculation based on correct principles is likely preferable to a certain and accurate calculation based on flawed reasoning.

Differences by Institution. Within the theoretical models set out here, different higher education institutions can face very different financial situations. For example, the level of available fixed revenue varies substantially across schools. A quick scan of different institutions' endowment assets quickly demonstrates this point (Strout, 2006). Schools without these fixed revenues have great difficulty engaging in activities central to their mission that do not generate sufficient revenue. McPherson and Schapiro (1998) understand this reality when they repeatedly state that the evaluations of an institution's commitment to need-based aid must incorporate considerations of the institution's financial situation. Institutions with greater levels of fixed revenues should certainly be expected to meet more of their students' needs. For need-based aid as well as other activities, institutional researchers must always consider the available level of financial resources when comparing their institution's performance against others.

To engage in important activities that run deficits, an institution with low fixed revenue must also identify and perform activities that produce profits. But schools with low fixed revenue may have trouble identifying profitable opportunities. Donors disproportionately give to the most prestigious institutions with the greatest existing financial strength. Federal and private research grants often go to schools with the strongest infrastructure and most renowned faculty. Essentially the conundrum is this: low fixed revenue increases the importance of engaging in profitable activities, but the available profitable activities diminish with the school's fixed revenue.

With these ideas in mind, recent findings demonstrating increased financial stratification across higher education institutions are not surprising. Winston (2004) finds that differences in spending per student across Carnegie classifications and between public and private institutions increased substantially between 1987 and 1996. This stratification may increase even more in the future because the richest private institutions are saving at drastically higher rates than other schools (Carbone and Winston, 2004).

Considerations for Specific Revenue Sources

An institution of higher education draws resources from numerous sources. Students and their families, the federal government, state governments, local governments, current donors, past donors (through endowment funds), and consumers from multiple contexts (patents, sporting events, and numerous other activities) all provide funds. Table 2.1 contains figures for the primary revenue sources for public and private institutions for the 1980–81 to 2000–01 period. Toutkoushian (2001, 2003) provides a thorough discussion and explanation of each individual revenue source, as well as the Higher Education General Information Survey (HEGIS) and the Integrated Postsecondary Education Data System (IPEDS) data used to produce these figures.

Table 2.1. General Revenue Shares by Source, 1980–81 to 2000–01

	1980–81	1985–86	1990–91	1995–96	1997–98	2000–01
Public institutions						
Tuition and fees	12.9	14.5	16.1	18.8	18.9	18.1
Federal government	12.8	10.5	10.3	11.1	10.6	11.2
State governments	45.6	45.0	40.3	35.8	35.7	35.6
Local governments	3.8	3.6	3.7	4.1	3.8	4.0
Private gifts, grants and contracts	2.5	3.2	3.8	4.1	4.5	5.1
Endowment income	0.5	0.6	0.5	0.6	0.6	0.8
Sales and services	19.6	20.0	22.7	22.2	22.2	21.7
Other sources	2.4	2.6	2.6	3.3	3.7	3.7
Private institutions						
Tuition and fees	35.9	37.8	39.4	41.5	27.8	38.1
Federal government	19.0	16.8	15.7	14.1	11.7	16.3
State governments	1.9	2.0	2.3	1.9	1.0	1.4
Local governments	0.8	0.6	0.7	0.7	0.5	0.6
Private gifts, grants and contracts	9.4	9.5	8.8	9.5	13.9	19.3
Endowment income	5.2	5.4	5.3	5.3		
Investment return					23.4	−4.4
Sales and services	23.5	23.7	23.3	21.6	17.4	23.5
Other sources	4.2	4.4	4.5	5.4	4.2	5.1

Notes: Figures taken from Table 332 of the 2002 Digest of Education Statistics (National Center for Education Statistics, 2002) and Table 332 and 338 of the 2004 Digest of Education Statistics (National Center for Education Statistics, 2004). The 1997–98 and 2000–01 figures for private institutions fundamentally differ from all other figures, because they are based on the new Financial Accounting Standards Board accounting.

Several differences across public and private institutions immediately become apparent. Public institutions rely much more heavily on state appropriations, while private institutions rely more on tuition and fees, private gifts, grants and contracts, and endowment income. But these differences are diminishing over time as the revenue shares for publics move toward the private model. Public institutions' state appropriation share decreased from 46 to 36 percent, while their private gifts, grants, and contracts share doubled and their tuition revenue share increased by 40 percent.

Two issues regarding the accounting standards used within higher education are worthy of note. First, these accounting standards have changed over time. After the 1995–96 fiscal year, the Financial Accounting Standards Board required private institutions to use a new accounting model that differed from the traditional model that both private and public institutions previously used (Budak, 2000). As a result, longitudinal examination of revenue shares for privates becomes more difficult, especially because the new accounting standards use investment return rather than endowment income, which leads to much greater variation across nearby years, as demonstrated by the 1997–98 and 2000–01 fiscal years in Table 2.1.

The accounting change also led to private institutions' reporting net tuition revenue as opposed to gross tuition revenue. The accounting standards that public institutions use for tuition revenue were similarly altered in 2002 by the General Accounting Standards Board. As I discuss later in this section, this change is quite important in principle. Furthermore, Toutkoushian (2001) demonstrates that net tuition revenue increased at slower rates than gross tuition revenue between 1984–85 and 1994–95, especially for private institutions. Except for the post 1995–96 figures for private institutions, the tuition and fee shares reported in Table 2.1 are for gross tuition revenue.

Regardless of the accounting standard used, the figures in Table 2.1 clearly demonstrate that tuition and fees are the primary revenue source for public institutions. And despite their decline over the period, state appropriations are still the primary revenue source for public institutions. Due to the importance of these two revenue sources, economists have devoted much more time to issues specific to them. As a result, I primarily examine these two sources in this part of the chapter. But I do mention several important considerations for other revenue sources, especially issues provoked by the above general discussion of revenues.

State Appropriations. Much has been written about how state appropriations to higher education have changed over the past thirty years. But this portrayal of how they have changed often varies substantially across articles. This inconsistency results from authors' using different measures, adjustments for inflation, and periods of study. An understanding of these complexities is important for any institutional researcher who wants to describe accurately how different revenue sources have changed over time for their institution.

The first measure used is the share of public institutions' revenues that come from state appropriations. Table 2.1 clearly demonstrates that state appropriations have fallen from this perspective. A similar finding occurs for the second measure, the share of state spending that flows to higher education. Kane, Orszag, and Gunter (2003) estimate that higher education spending went from 7.3 percent of state expenditures in 1977 to 5.3 percent in 2000.

The real complexity lies in the final measure used: the level of state funding per full-time-equivalent (FTE) student. This measure requires an adjustment for inflation and is extremely sensitive to the time period of study. Data from the 2003 *Digest of Education Statistics* (National Center for Education Statistics, 2003) and various years of the Grapevine Survey on State Tax Appropriations to Higher Education (Palmer, 2005) demonstrate these points.

If one examines the twenty-year period ending in the 2003–04 academic year, state appropriations per FTE student fell by 23 percent if one uses the Higher Education Price Index (HEPI) to adjust for inflation. But if the Consumer Price Index (CPI) is used instead, the drop is only 9 percent. The HEPI adjusts for changes in the price of those inputs commonly purchased by higher education institution, while the CPI considers goods bought by the typical consumer. Although the CPI is used in many published studies of state appropriations, most institutional researchers will find the HEPI to be more appropriate.

The estimated change in state appropriations also varies substantially across different periods of study. For example, state appropriations per FTE student increased by 2 percent between 1982–83 and 1998–99 using the HEPI, a very different result from the 23 percent drop between 1984–85 and 2003–04. This difference results from state appropriations that fluctuated tremendously in the short run with the health of the state economy. The years 1984–85 and 1998–99 were in periods of strong economic growth, while the years 1982–83 and 2003–04 were during poor economic times. Clearly institutional researchers should be extremely careful about making strong statements based on just two years of state appropriations data.

When multiple years are included in the analysis, state appropriations per FTE student do appear to be declining over time when the HEPI is being used. But the trend turns to stagnation when the CPI is used because the long-term trend does not reveal substantial growth or decline.

How might state appropriations change in the future? To answer this question, an understanding of the determinants of state funding for higher education is necessary. To describe the process by which state funding levels are chosen, economists have used several models from public economics. The median voter model, where the enacted policies reflect the preferences of the median voter, is the one most commonly used. The model contained in Becker (1983) provides a nice contrast, as it highlights how individual interest groups can have a disproportionate impact on chosen policies.

Using these theories, economists often specify a model of legislative demand for higher education. These models typically have higher education funding as a function of items such as the cost of higher education, the enrollments in the state, the size and wealth of the state, the tastes of the state for higher education, and the pressure within the state to spend on other government services. Although such models are relatively straightforward in theory, Rizzo (2004) and Toutkoushian and Hollis (1998) outline the numerous challenges that exist in terms of application to data.

From studies that have applied these models to data, the results of most interest regard the influence of competing spending priorities on higher education spending. Pressures to spend on K–12 education (Rizzo, 2004; Toutkoushian and Hollis, 1998) and Medicaid (Kane, Orszag, and Gunter, 2003) appear to lead to reduced funding for higher education. Because the required spending for these activities will likely increase in the future, especially for Medicaid, the state share spent on higher education is likely to decline even further. The amount that higher education institutions receive may be depressed still more by other factors such as the continued pressure on legislators not to increase taxes (Hovey, 1999), the structural deficits contained within the budgets of many state governments (Hovey, 1999; Jones,

2006), and the growing view among the public that higher education primarily produces private benefits (Selingo, 2003).

These changes have major consequences for public institutions because state appropriations traditionally have been used to support a range of activities that do not generate enough revenue to cover their costs. Consequently, these schools must seek to generate more revenue from their traditional activities, engage in new activities that generate profits, or reduce the costs of their traditional activities. The first option has often been used, especially for undergraduate and graduate education, as demonstrated by rising tuition and fee costs for many students.

Tuition Revenue. In the past, many higher education leaders viewed financial aid in a manner puzzling to economists. Institutional aid was deemed an expense, while gross tuition revenue, the listed tuition price multiplied by total enrollment, was implicitly thought to be a pool of revenue from which the institution could draw. From this perspective, leaders would be tempted to cap the spending on institutional aid when their school faced financial pressure.

Numerous economists successfully argued, however, that such an approach was often flawed (Breneman, 1994; McPherson and Schapiro, 1998). To demonstrate, consider a nonselective school that charges $20,000 and is currently below capacity so that one hundred students could be added with very little cost. For this school, one hundred additional students would indeed be willing to attend but would demand $5,000 in institutional aid. From the above perspective, the school would not offer this aid because it would increase the financial aid budget by $500,000, which would put it well above its self-imposed limit on financial aid.

This spending limit was motivated by a desire to improve the financial situation of the institution, but the opposite effect would likely occur. Instead of saving $500,000 in costs, the school misses the opportunity to generate $1.5 million in net tuition revenue. That increased revenue would have come at relatively little cost to the institution because it was substantially below capacity. The strength of this argument led to net tuition revenue becoming the primary measure used to examine tuition revenue, as demonstrated by the recent changes in accounting standards.

To this point, I have simply discussed higher education institutions in the aggregate, but Bowen and Breneman (1993) note that important differences exist between selective and nonselective institutions. For selective institutions, the treatment of institutional aid as a cost may not be problematic, because these institutions have an extended queue of students desiring enrollment and consequently are never under capacity. So enrolling a student needing large amounts of financial aid presents a real monetary cost: the missed opportunity to enroll a student who would pay full tuition. Bowen and Breneman (1993) call institutional aid an educational investment for this case, because revenue is forgone to ensure the school has a student body possessing certain characteristics.

NEW DIRECTIONS FOR INSTITUTIONAL RESEARCH • DOI: 10.1002/ir

For nonselective institutions, Bowen and Breneman (1993) describe institutional aid as a price discount, a term borrowed from microeconomic theory. Because these schools cannot fill their capacity simply by enrolling students paying full tuition, no revenue is forgone by offering financial aid. Consequently, the only cost of enrolling an additional student requiring financial aid is the marginal cost associated with his or her instruction.

To describe price discounting, economists typically specify the demand curve facing the organization, as shown in Figure 2.1 (Frank, 1997; Mankiw, 2001). The line D_E represents the demand curve for the potential incoming class of qualified students for a nonselective institution. The students are lined up on the horizontal axis in descending order by their willingness to pay for an enrollment slot at the school in question, and their position on the vertical axis represents the largest amount they are willing to pay.

If an institution has a listed tuition price of T_1 and provides no institutional aid, then it will enroll only E_1 students and generate net tuition revenue equal to the area of the rectangle created by the area T_1AE_10. If the school has a capacity that permits E_2 students, a large share of that capacity will go unused. The institution could simply lower tuition to T_2 to fill the unused capacity, but the net tuition revenue now falls to the area of the rectangle created by the area $T_2D_EE_20$. Alternatively, price discounting allows a school to simultaneously fill the unused capacity at the same time that it increases net tuition revenue. An institution can leave tuition at T_1 and offer aid to all students who are not willing to pay that price. The financial aid offers must be at least T_1 minus the highest price that the student of interest is willing to pay.

Figure 2.1. Revenue Implications of Price Discounting

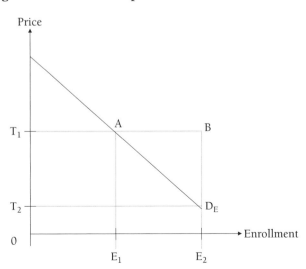

If an institution has a listed tuition price of T_1 and provides no institutional aid, then it will enroll only E_1 students and generate net tuition revenue equal to the area OT_1AE_1. If the school has a capacity that permits E_2 students, a large share of that capacity will go unused. The institution could simply lower tuition to T_2 to fill the unused capacity, but the net tuition revenue now falls to the area $OT_2D_EE_2$. Alternatively, price discounting allows a school to simultaneously fill the unused capacity at the same time that it increases net tuition revenue. An institution can leave tuition at T_1 and offer aid to all students who are not willing to pay that price. The financial aid offers must be at least T_1 minus the highest price that the student of interest is willing to pay.

With price discounting, a school now generates net tuition revenue equal to area $OT_1AD_EE_2$ and provides institutional aid equal to triangular area ABD_E (see Figure 2.1). Each student would add to the resources available to the institution as long as T_2 (the lowest net price paid by any student) is greater than the marginal cost of an additional student.

Once again, the seasoned institutional researcher may identify several aspects of the theoretical model that do not easily apply to practice. Most noticeably, the model assumes that financial aid officers can exactly measure a student's willingness to pay, when in reality an educated guess is the only tool available. Consequently, schools likely offer too much or too little aid to many of their potential students. In other words, they will not be able to perfectly price-discriminate. But even imperfect price discrimination may be preferable to extremely low listed tuition prices or unused capacity, and the imperfections in price discrimination will be lessened by the large amounts of relevant data that financial aid officers have on individual students.

A willingness to offer financial aid to any individual student as long as the net tuition paid is greater than marginal cost can potentially backfire if students become aware of this approach. If all students effectively negotiate their price toward marginal cost, the average revenue received from students may approach marginal cost. But marginal cost pricing is not sustainable because most higher education institutions have substantial fixed costs (Martin, 2002, 2004). Consequently, tuition discounting based on negotiation with individual students may not raise sufficient revenue in the long run.

Indeed, the large amount of discounting that is currently taking place has raised concern for the financial stability of many higher education institutions (Redd, 2000). Recent data for private colleges and universities show that approximately 80 percent of incoming freshmen in the fall of 2004 received some institutional aid, and the freshman discount rate, the institutional aid divided by gross tuition revenue, was close to 39 percent (Hubbell and Lapovsky, 2005). These figures represent substantial increases over past years; the corresponding figures for the fall of 1990, for example, were 62 and 26 percent, respectively (Hubbell and Lapovsky, 2005). The large discount rates do not purely reflect price discrimination, but also reflect other pressures that institutions face that are beyond the scope of this chapter, such as meeting financial need for low-income students and the competition across schools for students with strong academic credentials. When combined, these factors have resulted in institutions' receiving a smaller share of gross tuition dollars.

The discussion to this point has simply taken the listed tuition price as given. But the listed tuition price has increased substantially, almost doubling over the past twenty years in real terms, so that net tuition revenue increased at most institutions despite the large growth in institutional aid (College Board, 2005). The increasing discount rates simply moderated the amount of revenue generated.

Such realities are quite important for institutional researchers that are attempting to produce future estimates of net tuition revenue. Steven Corey and I are currently conducting research that examines a central issue in this area: How much extra net tuition revenue per student is generated by an increase in the listed tuition price? We expect our empirical estimates to suggest that net tuition revenues will increase at smaller rates than the listed tuition price.

Figure 2.2 demonstrates the reasoning underlying our hypothesis. If an institution increases its tuition price from T_1 to T_3, the amount of extra net tuition revenue generated is represented by the area $T_1 T_3 CF$; the amount of extra institutional aid required is represented by the area $FCDE$. Comparing Figure 2.2 to Figure 2.1 clearly demonstrates that the tuition increase will generate relatively little net tuition revenue.

Institutional researchers must clearly communicate this key point, because this information is extremely important for higher education leaders

Figure 2.2. Impact of Tuition Increases on Net Tuition Revenue

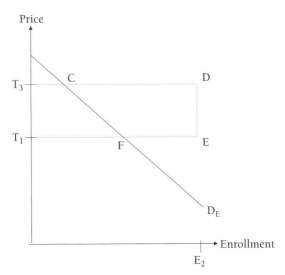

to understand. The public debate over tuition prices is based solely on the listed tuition price, and policymakers increasingly are pressuring colleges and universities not to increase listed tuition prices at rates higher than inflation. The above discussion, however, suggests that such small rises in the listed tuition price will generate increases in net tuition revenue that are well below inflation.

Other Revenue Sources. Given the declining role of state appropriations and the public pressure to cap tuition increases, many institutions of higher education increasingly will turn to other sources of revenue to improve their financial position. The available sources of revenue differ substantially in their ability to produce positive net revenue, and I discuss the profitability of some of the most prominent sources here.

Private gifts are an extremely attractive revenue source because the average cost per dollar raised is around sixteen cents (Ehrenberg, 2000). Hence, substantial positive net revenue can be generated. But restrictions on the gift can sometimes reduce its ability to subsidize other activities. If the restriction calls for the institution to engage in activities that it would not in the absence of the gift, then no new funds are available to subsidize the existing activities performed by the institution. Furthermore, a gift of this sort could actually increase the financial pressures of the institution if it does not fully cover the recurring costs of the new activities.

Great differences exist across institutions in their ability to obtain gifts, as certain schools have a larger pool of willing donors. Unfortunately, schools with the greatest need for additional dollars usually face the smallest pool of donors. For example, donors disproportionately give to those schools that already have the largest endowments.

A large endowment is the best indicator of a school on strong financial footing. Such assets produce consistent revenue that can subsidize a variety of activities deemed most important by the institution. Sizable endowments are impressive, but they are relatively rare within higher education. In 2005, approximately twenty-five schools had endowments above $2 billion, thirty had endowments between $1 and $2 billion, and fifty had endowments between $0.5 and $1 billion (Strout, 2006). The large majority of schools have endowments below $100 million.

To understand the importance of a large endowment, consider the case of a school with an enrollment of ten thousand students. If that school had a $2 billion endowment and drew from those assets yearly at a 4 percent payout rate, it could subsidize students' education by eight thousand dollars per student. Clearly these funds allow a school to gain a strong competitive advantage over other institutions and engage in a variety of socially important activities that do not generate substantial revenue.

Endowment assets also allow an institution to improve its research infrastructure, which can help it gain access to a variety of research grants. The extent to which research grants help the institution's financial situation is similar to private donations in that it varies by the specifics of the grant.

NEW DIRECTIONS FOR INSTITUTIONAL RESEARCH • DOI: 10.1002/ir

On one end of the spectrum are grants that fully cover indirect costs—that is, not only the direct costs of the funded research but also help in covering the costs associated with the general research infrastructure of the institution. As a result, the grant allows the institution to invest further in its research infrastructure or frees up funds for other activities. Grants that do not cover indirect costs can reduce the amount of dollars available for other activities if they also do not fully cover the direct costs of the grant. In this situation, the grant should fit squarely within the mission of the institution in order to be justified.

Higher education institutions are increasingly engaging in a variety of new entrepreneurial activities, but we know little yet about the extent to which such activities actually generate positive net revenue. The case of patent revenue suggests that profits may not always be forthcoming. Commercial research is often viewed as a promising source of revenues, given the overall magnitude of dollars involved. In fiscal year 2004, over $1 billion in revenues were collected from licenses on a variety of inventions by professors and students (Blumenstyk, 2005).

But Ehrenberg, Rizzo, and Jakubson (2003) note that these figures greatly overestimate the extent to which patent revenue can help improve the financial position of a typical institution. Licensing income is highly skewed, with 8 of the 164 institutions surveyed enjoying more than half of all revenues reported in 2004 (Blumenstyk, 2005). Furthermore, any revenues generated are divided between the university and the researchers. The institution's share of the revenues must then cover the substantial development and legal costs required for these activities. After taking these considerations into account, Ehrenberg, Rizzo, and Jakubson (2003) find that a considerable number of schools lose money on technology transfer initiatives, and the amount of dollars earned at many profitable institutions is relatively modest.

Conclusion

The primary goal of this chapter was to provide institutional researchers with an economic framework that allows them to understand the contribution of each revenue source to the financial position of the institution. The framework, relatively simple in theory, requires answers to several key questions: Which activities produce positive net revenue, and how large are these profits? Which activities produce negative net revenue, and how large are these deficits? How much fixed revenue is generated?

Despite the simplicity of this framework in theory, the application to data presents numerous challenges. Partially for this reason, the research literature has rarely produced clear answers to these questions. Nevertheless, such knowledge is increasingly important. The justification for many recent policy decisions at the institution and government level implicitly assumes that a variety of activities can produce substantial positive net revenue. But too often those assumptions are based on aggregate national data, as in the case for patent revenue, as opposed to careful analysis of data from individual institutions of higher education.

Institutional researchers are perhaps the best-placed individuals to perform this analysis. A major impediment to such research in the past has been the scarcity of publicly available data with sufficient information to evaluate the economic contribution of each individual activity. Many researchers were also limited by insufficient knowledge of the context and accounting practices of the institutions under study. But institutional researchers do not face these limitations. They have access to detailed institutional data and have a firm understanding of the institutions within which they work.

References

Becker, G. "A Theory of Competition Among Pressure Groups for Political Influence." *Quarterly Journal of Economics,* 1983, *98*(3), 371–400.

Blumenstyk, G. "Colleges Cash In on Commercial Activity." *Chronicle of Higher Education,* Dec. 2, 2005, p. 25.

Bok, D. *Universities in the Marketplace: The Commercialization of Higher Education.* Princeton, N.J.: Princeton University Press, 2003.

Bowen, H. *The Costs of Higher Education: How Much Do Colleges and Universities Spend per Student and How Much Should They Spend?* San Francisco: Jossey-Bass, 1980.

Bowen, W., and Breneman, D. "Student Aid: Price Discount or Educational Investment?" *Brookings Review,* 1993, *11*(1), 28–31.

Breneman, D. *Liberal Arts Colleges: Thriving, Surviving, or Endangered?* Washington, D.C.: Brookings Institution, 1994.

Budak, S. "IPEDS Finance Data Comparisons Under the 1997 Financial Accounting Standards for Private, Not-for-Profit Institutes: A Concept Paper." Washington, D.C.: U.S. Department of Education, Office of Educational Research and Improvement, 2000.

Cantor, N., and Courant, P. "Scrounging for Resources: Reflections on the Whys and Wherefores of Higher Education Finance." In F. Alexander and R. Ehrenberg (eds.), *Maximizing Revenue in Higher Education.* New Directions for Institutional Research, no. 119. San Francisco: Jossey-Bass, 2003.

Carbone, J., and Winston, G. "Saving, Wealth, Performance, and Revenues in U.S. Colleges and Universities." *Review of Higher Education,* 2004, *28*(1), 97–128.

College Board. *Trends in College Pricing.* New York: College Board, 2005.

Ehrenberg, R. *Tuition Rising: Why College Costs So Much.* Cambridge, Mass.: Harvard University Press, 2000.

Ehrenberg, R., Rizzo, M., and Jakubson, G. "Who Bears the Growing Cost of Science at Universities?" Cambridge, Mass.: National Bureau of Economic Research, 2003.

Frank, R. *Microeconomics and Behavior.* (3rd ed.) New York: McGraw-Hill, 1997.

Hovey, H. "State Spending for Higher Education in the Next Decade: The Battle to Sustain Current Support." San Jose, Calif.: National Center for Public Policy and Higher Education, 1999.

Hubbell, L., and Lapovsky, L. "Tuition Discounting: Fifteen Years in Perspective." 2005. Retrieved May 15, 2006, from http://www.nacubo.org/x6363.xml.

James, E. "Product Mix and Cost Disaggregation: A Reinterpretation of the Economics of Higher Education." *Journal of Human Resources,* 1978, *13*(2), 157–186.

James, E., and Neuberger, E. "The University Department as a Non-Profit Labor Cooperative." *Public Choice,* 1981, *36*(3), 585–612.

Jones, D. "State Shortfalls Projected to Continue Despite Economic Gains: Long-Term Prospects for Higher Education No Brighter." San Jose, Calif.: National Center for Public Policy and Higher Education, 2006.

Kane, T., Orszag, P., and Gunter, D. "State Fiscal Constraints and Higher Education Spending: The Role of Medicaid and the Business Cycle." Washington, D.C.: Urban Institute, 2003.

Mankiw, N. *Principles of Economics.* (2nd ed.) Orlando, Fla.: Harcourt, 2001.

Martin, R. "Tuition Discounting: Theory and Evidence." *Economics of Education Review,* 2002, *21*(2), 125–136.

Martin, R. "Tuition Discounting Without Tears." *Economics of Education Review,* 2004, *23*(2), 177–189.

McPherson, M., and Schapiro, M. *The Student Aid Game: Meeting Need and Rewarding Talent in American Higher Education.* Princeton, N.J.: Princeton University Press, 1998.

National Center for Education Statistics, U.S. Department of Education. *Digest of Education Statistics 2002.* 2002. Retrieved May 15, 2006, from http://nces.ed.gov/programs/digest/d02/.

National Center for Education Statistics, U.S. Department of Education. *Digest of Education Statistics 2003.* 2003. Retrieved Apr. 19, 2005, from http://nces.ed.gov/programs/digest/d03/.

National Center for Education Statistics, U.S. Department of Education. *Digest of Education Statistics 2004.* 2004. Retrieved May 15, 2006, from http://nces.ed.gov/programs/digest/d04/.

Palmer, J. *Grapevine, An Annual Compilation of Data on State Tax Appropriation for the General Operation of Higher Education.* Retrieved Apr. 19, 2005, from http://www.grapevine.ilstu.edu/.

Redd, K. "Discounting Toward Disaster: Tuition Discounting, College Finances, and Enrollments of Low-Income Undergraduates." Indianapolis, Ind.: USA Group Foundation, 2000.

Rizzo, M. "A (Less Than) Zero Sum Game? State Funding for Public Higher Education: How Public Higher Education Institutions Have Lost." Unpublished doctoral dissertation, Cornell University, 2004.

Selingo, J. "What Americans Think About Higher Education." *Chronicle of Higher Education,* May 2, 2003, p. 10.

Slaughter, S., and Rhoades, G. *Academic Capitalism and the New Economy: Markets, State and Higher Education.* Baltimore, Md.: Johns Hopkins University Press, 2004.

Strout, E. "College Endowments Post 'Respectable' Returns for 2005." *Chronicle of Higher Education,* Jan. 27, 2006, p. B1.

Toutkoushian, R. "Trends in Revenues and Expenditures for Public and Private Higher Education." In M. Paulsen and J. Smart (eds.), *The Finance of Higher Education: Theory, Research, Policy, and Practice.* New York: Agathon Press, 2001.

Toutkoushian, R. "Weathering the Storm: Generating Revenues for Higher Education During a Recession." In F. Alexander and R. Ehrenberg (eds.), *Maximizing Revenue in Higher Education.* New Directions for Institutional Research, no. 119. San Francisco: Jossey-Bass, 2003.

Toutkoushian, R., and Hollis, P. "Using Panel Data to Examine Legislative Demand for Higher Education." *Education Economics,* 1998, *6*(2), 141–57.

Winston, G. "Differentiation Among U.S. Colleges and Universities." *Review of Industrial Organization,* 2004, *24*(4), 331–54.

Zemsky, R., Wegner, G., and Massy, W. *Remaking the University: Market-Smart and Mission-Centered.* New Brunswick, N.J.: Rutgers University Press, 2005.

JOHN J. CHESLOCK *is assistant professor of higher education at the Center for the Study of Higher Education, University of Arizona.*

NEW DIRECTIONS FOR INSTITUTIONAL RESEARCH • DOI: 10.1002/ir

3

Economics provides fertile ground, both theoretical and empirical, for institutional researchers interested in higher education costs.

Using Economic Concepts in Institutional Research on Higher Education Costs

Paul T. Brinkman

Institutional researchers are uniquely positioned to provide the information and advice needed to assist administrators and others in addressing a variety of issues involving college and university operating costs. Many other individuals on campus deal with those costs every day, including budget managers as well as accountants who record and document the institution's financial affairs. Such work is necessary and produces foundational data, but it is not sufficient. Could one reasonably expect cost accountants to address questions such as whether average costs per student were likely to change if the institution were to double in size or whether average costs were lower at other, similar institutions? The answer is clearly no. To address such questions entails not just budgeting or accounting for expenditures but connecting those expenditures to the appropriate inputs and outputs while being attentive to factors that might confound the analysis. It is institutional researchers who create the intersection of these various kinds of data, employ the appropriate analytical routines, and interpret and give meaning to the findings. Economics provides cost-related concepts, models, and empirical findings that can help institutional researchers in successfully undertaking these activities.

Institutional researchers have three tasks involving costs and cost analysis: understanding and explaining the nature of costs, determining costs, and interpreting and comparing costs. I comment briefly on each of those

NEW DIRECTIONS FOR INSTITUTIONAL RESEARCH, no. 132, Winter 2006 © Wiley Periodicals, Inc.
Published online in Wiley InterScience (www.interscience.wiley.com) • DOI: 10.1002/ir.195

tasks, discuss the rudiments of the economic model of costs, examine how the economic model and empirical cost studies relate to those tasks, and reflect on how the economic model can be used to identify some of the reasons that higher education costs continue to increase.

This chapter focuses almost entirely on institutional operating costs. Two important types of cost are not discussed here: the cost of facilities, or capital costs, and the costs borne by students.

Cost-Related Tasks for Institutional Researchers

There is good reason that institutional researchers need to understand and be able to explain the nature of costs. Administrators may need their assistance in dealing with costs during the annual budget cycle, especially in years when budget cuts are called for or when significant new money is available. Advice on costs will likely be needed when the campus is engaged in strategic planning and possibly contemplating changes in the size or the mission of the institution. Administrators are likely to need help as they discuss costs with external audiences who are entitled to know something of the institution's operating costs and the reasons behind those costs.

The supportive role of the institutional researcher in this context may entail helping to frame the discussion rather than solely providing cost figures. It may entail casting the local experience either within a conceptual framework or in relation to findings from the research literature. Economics provides established ways of thinking that are useful for framing a discussion of costs, as well as numerous empirical studies that document actual cost behavior, thus serving as a multifaceted resource for institutional researchers in their advisory role.

The first step in determining, or measuring, costs is to decide what type of cost is most appropriate. There are many kinds of costs. Some will be relevant in a given situation, and others will not. For example, a department's current cost per student may not be the best indicator of future costs should enrollment change significantly. The second step in determining costs is choosing and implementing the appropriate analytical method. Data issues, statistical routines, and various cost-finding principles will be in play. Observing how economists and econometricians have gone about their work in determining costs can provide helpful guidance.

A stand-alone cost figure is seldom interesting or informative in its own right. Interpretation and contextualization are usually needed to obtain full value and meaning. The institutional researcher can employ two related but different strategies to provide those elements. One is to examine a cost finding within a conceptual framework, which may suggest how the costs in question should behave or point to other dimensions or issues that warrant attention.

The other way to create meaning is to compare costs among operating units or across time. Such comparisons, particularly the former, are deceptively simple to make and can easily be either misleading or invalid. Economic concepts and the cost analysis strategies that economists employ can alert the researcher to potential threats to validity and suggest ways to mitigate those threats.

Economic Model of Costs

The word *cost* can mean different things to different people and is often used with a vague meaning. It is both a technical term in several disciplines and part of common parlance. From the economist's perspective the fundamental meaning of *cost* is always to be found in forgone opportunities. Those opportunities, in turn, depend on the options and constraints facing the relevant decision maker or decision-making organization.

As a rule, there is no single right answer to the question, "How much does this cost?" The appropriate answer depends on the context that gave rise to the question. The distinction between relevant and irrelevant costs will always depend on the specific choice or specific decision under analysis. "Different costs for different purposes" is the appropriate mantra. To generalize a bit more, it should also be kept in mind that costs are not some sort of abstract quantity. Costs are always someone's costs. In this chapter, the focus is on operating costs as experienced by administrators, as opposed to, for example, the opportunity costs experienced by faculty members in the process of producing instruction or research. The latter costs could be different from the amount (the supplier price) that faculty members charge the institution to provide the service. A wide-ranging discussion of the many different types of cost and cost analysis can be found in Brinkman and Allen (1986). Simpson and Sperber (1984) provide an example of a cost analysis that is focused on the use of resources, or opportunity costs, rather than on expenditures.

The production function and the cost function constitute the twin pillars of the economic model of costs. The production function represents the technology available to an organization, that is, the possible relationships between outputs (products and services) and inputs (labor, equipment, and facilities, for example). This function states the maximum output obtainable from every possible input combination (technical efficiency). The cost function represents the relationship between an organization's costs and its output rate (level of production). The organization's production technology and the prices it pays for inputs determine its cost function. The classical economist assumes that an organization will assemble and combine inputs in such a manner as to maximize output while minimizing costs (productive efficiency, the combination of technical and allocative efficiency).

Economists also assume that all inputs can be divided into two categories: fixed and variable. The quantity of a fixed input does not change as the rate of output changes, while the quantity of a variable input does change. Economists define the short run as that period in which there is at least one fixed input. The latter often consists of facilities or major equipment but could be some other input. By definition, all inputs are variable in the long run, including the physical plant. It is also assumed that the law of diminishing returns is operative in the short run. As equal increments of one input are added and the quantities of other inputs held constant, the marginal product of the input whose quantity is being increased will diminish.

Three concepts of total cost are important in the short run: total fixed cost, total variable cost, and total cost (the sum of fixed and variable cost). Also important are average fixed cost (total fixed cost divided by output), average variable cost (total variable cost divided by output), average total cost (total cost divided by output), and marginal cost (the change in total cost resulting from the addition of one unit of output). It is assumed that marginal cost, average total cost, and average variable cost are second-degree curves that first decline and then increase as output is expanded (Figure 3.1).

Economies and diseconomies of scale determine the shape of the long-run, average-cost curve. Returns to scale are increasing (decreasing) if a unit increases all inputs by the same proportion and output increases by more (less) than this proportion. Economies of scale are present any time the ratio of marginal cost to average total cost is less than one. Whether there are constant, increasing, or decreasing returns to scale is an empirical question to be decided on a case-by-case basis. The shape of the long-run average cost curve in a particular industry is important for public policy insofar as that policy can influence the number and size of firms in an industry.

Figure 3.1. Average and Marginal Cost Curves

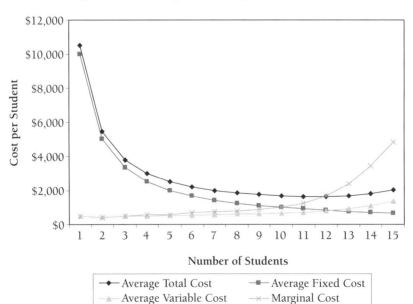

Economists pay considerable attention to organizations that have multiple outputs, including outputs that can be produced jointly. Issues that arise include economies of scope, the possibility that two or more products can be produced more efficiently jointly rather than separately, and single-product returns to scale versus ray, or combined-product, returns to scale.

More extensive presentations of the economic model of costs can be found in any microeconomics textbook. Hoenack (1990) provides an insightful discussion of how an economist uses the model in thinking about higher education costs.

Determining Costs

Costs can be estimated statistically, calculated, engineered, constructed, or even negotiated. In what follows, we look at two approaches that economists have used frequently in determining college and university operating costs. In one approach, the preferred method for most econometricians, cost behavior is estimated using cost functions. The other approach, which has also been used to good purpose by economists, is the straightforward, but careful, calculation of average costs. The first requires more statistical skills. Both require attention in order to conceptualize and structure the analysis properly.

Shapes and Relationships. The cost function is the most useful tool for analyzing the economic behavior of organizations. In this section, the focus is on its use in estimating the shape of cost curves, that is, the relationship between costs and the rate of output, and for assessing cost-related correlations among outputs.

Estimating a cost function involves a statistical technique (some form of least-squares estimator such as ordinary least squares), a model (an estimating equation, or function), and time-series or, more often, cross-sectional data. Cost (total or average) is regressed on output, input prices, and technical conditions (other factors that affect costs). Ideally the analyst can specify the correct form of the function, based on knowledge of the underlying production process. Economists do not agree on which functional form is the most appropriate, which is unfortunate because marginal cost estimates in particular are very sensitive to functional form. It is clear that some forms are inappropriate. Consider a function in which total costs in raw dollars are regressed on a single raw, first-order variable (no squared or cubic or logarithmic terms) representing output. The estimated coefficient on that variable, an estimate of marginal cost, will perforce be a constant. By choosing that particular functional form, the analyst misses the chance to actually test for the shape of the cost curve.

Economists conceptualize the total cost curve as representing the expansion path of the fully efficient firm. The optimization assumption is problematic when applied to colleges and universities. Most observers would agree that the intent and ability to minimize costs is largely missing in higher education. Accordingly, the coefficients estimated in higher education cost functions are perhaps best characterized as reflecting average behavior rather than technological imperatives. This does not, however, make those estimates any less valuable for the institutional researcher seeking an understanding of cost behavior, as the following illustrative studies demonstrate.

Toutkoushian (1999) estimates a variety of cost functions designed to examine economies of scale and scope and other factors likely to influence the cost of production in colleges and universities. The dependent variable in his multiple regression models is either total expenditures or total expenditures divided by number of students (that is, average cost per student), where total expenditures includes instruction, academic support, student services, institutional support, plant operations, and transfers. Three independent variables represent output: number of undergraduate students, number of graduate students, and research dollars (awards) received. These variables are entered in the regression equation in cubic and quadratic forms to allow for variability in marginal and average costs in relationship to volume of output (that is, to allow scale effects to be discovered if present). Output variables are also interacted with one another to reveal possible economies of scope. The use of interaction terms in this manner is common practice, although the procedure does not distinguish between results based on technological requirements and those based on deliberate choice (James, 1978). Average salary for full professors is the variable used to control for variation in input prices. Various technical conditions are also represented in the equation, including the student-faculty ratio, the percentage of faculty in the full professor rank, the percentage of expenditures devoted to instruction, geographical and urban location, and public versus private control. The model does not control for programmatic differences except that institutions with medical schools are excluded. The sample analyzed contains 828 four-year institutions.

Toutkoushian finds evidence for a U-shaped average cost curve for undergraduate enrollment, holding graduate enrollment, research award dollars, and the other variables in the model constant. Minimum cost per student is reached at twenty-three thousand undergraduates, suggesting that most four-year institutions could lower their average costs by expanding undergraduate enrollment. As Toutkoushian points out, however, many other issues are at stake in considering the optimal size of particular institutions. This is also true of systems of public institutions where, for example, smaller, less efficient institutions may be needed in order to provide access for place-bound students. It should also be noted that research findings regarding the effects of scale are inconsistent. Although many studies have found evidence for economies of scale, some have not; references and commentary on this issue can be found in Toutkoushian (1999), Brinkman and Leslie (1986), and Brinkman (1990). Perhaps the inconsistency is not surprising given that the various studies differ with respect to the form of the cost function, the dependent and independent variables, and the samples analyzed. Enrollment changes that occur near the time when average cost is measured can distort estimates of scale effects (Getz and Siegfried,

1991; Harter, Wade, and Watkins, 2005). Institutional researchers need to consider all of these facets in evaluating the applicability of a particular finding to their local situation.

Toutkoushian also provides evidence for economies of scale for research and for economies of scope between research and graduate instruction and between research and undergraduate instruction, but not between the two levels of instruction. In other words, his estimates indicate that it is less expensive to produce research and either graduate or undergraduate instruction jointly rather than separately. Finally, his model indicates, not surprisingly, that the student-faculty ratio and average faculty salaries have a heavy impact on average costs, holding all other variables constant.

Dundar and Lewis (1995) estimate a cost function to analyze the cost structures of three departmental clusters (physical sciences, social sciences, and engineering) across eighteen public research universities. They find evidence of ray economies of scale for all three clusters, meaning that departments would accrue cost efficiencies from producing more output (undergraduate, master's, and doctoral-level instruction, and research) in fixed proportions. They also find evidence of economies of scope, but these relationships differ depending on the discipline. For example, economies of scope are found between doctoral and undergraduate teaching (number of credit hours) in the social sciences but not in the physical sciences and engineering. The authors speculate that this result is due to a difference in the way that doctoral students are used, in the former instance as teachers and in the latter instance as fellow researchers. Conversely, economies of scope exist between research (number of publications) and doctoral teaching in the physical sciences and engineering but not in the social sciences. The authors used graduate program rankings to control for possible differences in quality among the departments, but did not find a significant relationship between quality and departmental costs.

Average Costs. Average costs are calculated and reported more frequently than any other in higher education. A typical calculation is total instructional cost divided by total credit hours. This particular cost is often derived by institutional researchers for use in comparing costs among academic departments or among institutions. Analysts in state higher education agencies use average cost per student in making cost comparisons among institutions within state systems. Average costs are featured in national surveys, the Delaware Study of Costs and Productivity being a notable example, in which average costs are compared among similar departments or programs in different institutions (Middaugh, 2002).

Average cost can sometimes be calculated in a straightforward, simple manner, as when the analysis is limited to direct costs incurred by a cost center that produces a single type of output. Average costs are more difficult to calculate when the task involves tracking direct costs through multiple cost centers, as will likely be the case when the unit of analysis is a process such as recruiting students or producing a degree. Average costs must be estimated rather than calculated when multiple outputs are produced simultaneously by the same inputs. Another kind of difficulty arises when the analyst must allocate indirect (support) costs to outputs in a multiple output situation. For example, in a university setting, how should the cost of operating the library or the cost of administrative overhead be allocated to undergraduate education, graduate education, research, and public service, respectively? Hyatt (1983) provides a discussion and possible allocation schemes, as do Rooney, Borden, and Thomas (1997). Allocating the cost of capital facilities across multiple, jointly produced outputs would present similar difficulties.

Variations in average cost per credit hour by discipline typically are large because of differences by discipline in input prices and production functions (input requirements, input utilization). Consider, for example, the key input price, faculty salaries. Average salaries in one discipline, such as accounting, may be much higher than comparable salaries in another discipline, such as history. As for the production function, consider how different input-output relationships are among the disciplines of nursing (with restrictions on the number of students on a hospital ward), mechanical engineering (with major equipment requirements), and sociology (with no class size restrictions and no major equipment requirements). Middaugh (2005) demonstrates the wide variation in average cost per student among disciplines.

Harter, Wade, and Watkins (2005) focus on changes in average costs per student over time across a variety of types of four-year public colleges and universities (376 in all). Their analysis, which extends earlier work by Getz and Siegfried (1991), examines the change from 1989–1990 to 1998–1999 in average, real (adjusted for inflation) expenditures per student in different functional areas, such as instruction and academic support, by type of institution. They also examine the effect of changes in enrollment on total expenditures per student, as well as the relationship between the rate of growth in total expenditures per student and growth rates in instructional expenditures, faculty salary expenditures, the number of faculty, and full-time-equivalent (FTE) enrollment.

They found that expenditures for instruction and plant operations declined in relative importance for all institutional types between 1989 and 1998, while expenditures for academic support and student services increased in relative importance. Real overall expenditures per FTE student increased over the period by 2.02 percent per year for institutions without medical schools and by 2.37 percent for institutions with medical schools. Among all institutional types, the highest annual growth rate, 3.57 percent, was experienced by doctoral institutions with medical schools; the lowest rate, 1.73 percent, occurred at comprehensive institutions without medical schools and more than ten thousand FTE students. Obviously institutional type made a difference, demonstrating the risks of a one-size-fits-all mindset in discussing average costs per student in higher education.

Direct calculation is not the only option for addressing average costs. As we saw earlier, cost functions can be used to estimate the shape of the average cost curve, the relationship between cost and the level of output. Those same functions can be used to estimate relationships between average costs and other dimensions subject to institutional policies. For example, Toutkoushian (1999) finds that increasing the student-faculty ratio by one would result in a decline of $170 in average cost per student. He also quantifies the impact on costs of faculty salaries and the distribution of faculty by rank.

Marginal Costs. While the concept of marginal cost, the change in total cost accompanying an additional unit of output, may not be as familiar as that of average cost, it is at least as useful. Marginal costs (and marginal benefits) are relevant when deciding where to allocate incremental resources. They are useful when designing funding formulas, whether for institutions as a whole or for units within institutions. These costs are useful too when considering whether growth is appropriate from a financial perspective. For example, in contemplating the value of increased enrollment, it is worth asking whether marginal costs will equal or exceed the revenue gained per additional student enrolled. It does not make sense conceptually to rely on average costs for guidance in these situations, whereas reliance on marginal costs is appropriate. As illustrated in Figure 3.1, they can differ materially from average costs. Brinkman (1990) reviews a variety of higher education cost studies in which marginal costs are shown to be less than average costs.

Determining marginal costs normally requires large amounts of data and the use of statistical estimation techniques. Toutkoushian (1999), for example, uses his cost functions to provide estimates of marginal costs. He finds wide variations in marginal costs by level of enrollment, institutional type, and institutional control. This is yet another example of the versatility of cost functions; they can and often are used to estimate marginal costs. Note too that when the log of total cost is regressed on the log of output, the log-log functional form, the resulting coefficient represents the estimated ratio of marginal to average costs (Brinkman, 1985).

A researcher could attempt to calculate directly the relationship between small changes in the quantity of output and changes in total costs. There is little likelihood, however, that such changes will behave consistently in a theoretically reasonably manner (Allen and Brinkman, 1983). In the microcosm of a single department or program or institution, total costs could as easily go down or up, not so much in response to, but in temporal association with, a change of one unit of production, such as an additional student taught. One could, of course, observe the relationship between changes in annual output (for example, enrollment or degrees awarded) and changes in the annual budget (in constant dollars). There is no guarantee that such incremental costs will behave as theory might predict, but the issue is an empirical one and the results might be interesting.

Fixed versus Variable Costs. Distinguishing between fixed and variable costs is yet another way to address the relationship between costs and the quantity of output, the focal relationship in the economic model of costs. Considering fixed and variable costs is useful for a wide variety of budgeting, planning, and management control purposes. Among other things, it is a way to address scale effects. The presence of at least some fixed costs ensures the likelihood of positive returns to scale over some range of production (see Figure 3.1). As production increases, only the variable portion of total cost increases, which means that average total cost will decrease over some range of increased output in most circumstances. If all costs are fixed, marginal cost will be zero. When some costs are variable, average variable costs can be used as an estimate of marginal cost across some portion of the range of output.

Fixed and *variable* are not synonyms for *uncontrollable* and *controllable* costs. Controllable costs are those that can be affected by management action; uncontrollable costs cannot be so affected. The concept of variability relates primarily to the technical nature of the production process, while the concept of controllability relates primarily to the scope for management action.

Determining what is a fixed cost versus what is a variable cost often involves examining a mix of policies, strategies, negotiations, and technical considerations. Consider the issue in relation to class size. What is the appropriate size for a writing section, a calculus section, a history section, a lab section, or a health care practicum? Only in the last two cases are we likely to encounter technical limits (constraints on the number of students allowed into the section) apart from the occasional space limitation. In the other cases, pedagogical and personal preferences tend to dictate which input-output relationships are allowable, as heads of academic units and their faculties negotiate with one another within some framework of discipline-base mores and incentives. Institutional researchers tasked with distinguishing fixed from variable costs would be well advised to concentrate on understanding the actors and the decision processes as much as technical considerations.

Interpreting and Comparing Costs

Institutional researchers can and should play a key role in making sense of, and adding meaning to, cost data. Comparing costs either by cross-section or over time is the most frequently used approach to accomplishing this task, but there is danger here, especially in regard to cross-sectional comparisons. Anyone can assemble a set of institutions or academic departments, divide expenditures by the number of students, and compare the results. If such comparisons are done poorly, they do more harm than good.

For example, it is easy to conceive of a situation in which misleading conclusions are drawn through inattention to multiple outputs. Imagine two institutions where instruction and research are produced jointly. Each institution has total faculty expenditures of $6 million, 2,000 students, and 20 units of research production. Institution A allocates an estimated 90 percent of faculty time to instruction and 10 percent to research. Institution A's total faculty instructional cost, then, is $5.4 million, and its average cost per student is $2,700. Its total faculty research cost is $600,000, with an average cost per unit of $30,000. Institution B allocates an estimated 80 percent of faculty time to instruction and 20 percent to research, which yields $4.8 million in total faculty instructional cost, an average cost per student of $2,400, total faculty research cost of $1.2 million, with an average cost per unit of $60,000. While literally true, it would be misleading to report only that institution A spends more per student than institution B, and leave it at that. But the picture is more complicated and more nuanced than the instructional cost figures alone portray. Institutional researchers need to recognize those subtleties and help others understand them.

As noted earlier, econometricians have developed procedures that can defeat or at least mitigate threats to validity, including the use of control variables in cost functions and the stratification of institutional or departmental samples. For example, by inserting a dummy variable for institutional control in his cost functions, Toutkoushian (1999) found that public institutions spend less per student than private institutions do after controlling for size, the student-faculty ratio, output rates, input prices, and the other independent variables. In this case, control is achieved by holding the independent variables constant at their mean values while examining the relationship between average cost per student and private versus public ownership.

Harter, Wade, and Watkins (2005) achieve a measure of control through sample stratification, an approach that may be particularly appropriate when working with lay audiences unfamiliar with multivariate statistical routines. They assemble groups of institutions that they have reason to believe will behave in similar fashion and then compare developments over time among the various groups. In this approach, analysts rely on their knowledge of factors that affect costs as they construct groups of similar institutions. Attention is paid to possible differences in output mix, input prices, and other conditions that might bear on costs. In other words, the focus is on the same set of dimensions that one might include in constructing the set of independent variables to use in a cost function, but in this instance, the variables point the way to constructing an appropriate set of comparators rather than exerting control within a statistical procedure.

In yet another approach to comparing average costs, Toutkoushian (1999) uses the estimated coefficients in his study to generate predicted average cost per student by institution. He compares the predicted cost to actual cost, calculates the gap, and rank-orders institutions by the size of the gap. By developing interinstitutional cost comparisons through the medium of the cost function, he controls for differences in the level of outputs and the other cost factors included in his model. The analyst needs to think carefully about what it means to make such comparisons while holding variables such as the student-faculty ratio and average faculty salaries constant, or, as in Toutkoushian's study, not holding constant the mix of programs offered. That said, institutional researchers can use this predicted-versus-actual approach to establish where their institution stands in terms of relative efficiency. A researcher in an institution deemed to be "high cost" when compared in more typical ways might look to this kind of analysis to determine whether the high costs are to be expected (predicted by the model) when various cost factors are taken into account. This approach to estimating relative efficiency complements that generated by frontier analyses such as data envelopment analysis (Johnes and Johnes, 1995).

Cost function studies, such as Toutkoushian's, and calculation routines, such as those in Harter, Wade, and Watkins, employ effective strategies for dealing with institutional differences that could confound or hide important findings. The two types of studies yield a wealth of information and complement one another well. Both shed light on reasons for the increase in average cost per student.

Increasing Costs

Costs have been an issue in higher education for a long time, and interest has intensified because of extraordinary increases in tuition, a price charged by an institution and a cost to students. It is important to note that increases in tuition do not necessarily imply increases in institutional operating costs because, in contrast to the private sector, price (tuition) does not equal cost plus markup. In higher education, tuition equals cost minus subsidy (principally state appropriations, gifts, and endowment earnings). Therefore, increases in tuition can be the result of decreases in subsidies rather than increases in operating costs. The lay public and some elected officials seem to have difficulty grasping this relationship and may need to be reminded of it. Transposing terms in the equation shows that cost equals tuition plus subsidy. Therefore, increases in tuition may permit increases in operating costs, depending on changes in subsidies.

Much has been said or written regarding cost increases in higher education (for example, Bowen, 1980; Brinkman 1992; Baumal and Blackman, 1995; Gumport and Pusser, 1995; Leslie and Rhoades, 1995; Clotfelter, 1996; Ehrenberg, 2000; Morphew and Baker, 2004; Middaugh, 2005; Harter, Wade, and Watkins, 2005), including a special study at the behest of Congress (National Commission on the Cost of Higher Education, 1998). As these studies amply demonstrate, there are many reasons that operating costs might increase and many different approaches to understanding the phenomenon. In what follows, the focus is on reasons and approaches that are related to the cost concepts discussed earlier in the chapter.

The concern about costs is not about the total cost of higher education but about average cost per student. Conceptually an institution experiences a change in average cost either because its entire average cost curve moves up or down or because the institution moves along the average cost curve in response to a change in the quantity of output. Movement of the cost curve itself could be the result of a change in input prices or a change in the production function, the relationship between inputs and outputs.

As for input prices, higher education experiences some of the same pressures, for example, from rising energy and health care costs, as do other industries. By contrast, increases in the prices paid for library resources are more telling for colleges and universities than elsewhere. Input prices overall for higher education have historically outpaced general price inflation (Layzell and Caruthers, 2002). Individual institutions can incur increased input prices depending on choices they make. For example, hiring and retaining renowned faculty or faculty in disciplines where demand outstrips supply will lead to higher average cost per student even as the number of faculty remains constant, while substituting part-time for full-time faculty will result in lower rather than higher cost per student.

There is at least one obvious example of a production function change that has led to higher average cost per student and can be found on every campus: the revolution in information technology, which adds significantly to both labor and capital inputs even when output, the number of students, remains constant. Consider the increase in the number of personal computers, printers, and other computer devices such as scanners and remote sensors over the past several decades, from a handful to thousands or even tens of thousands on a typical campus. Large universities spend millions of dollars annually to keep its computer hardware up to date. Since those computers need to be maintained, protected, housed, powered, equipped with software, connected to a broadband network, and in many cases accompanied by portals and Web sites, the true cost of this complex set of technological innovations is actually much greater than a renewal and replacement budget for hardware would suggest. This is not just about equipment. For example, the number of Webmasters on the typical campus is significant. This particular job did not exist a short time ago, nor have these particular specialists replaced other employees whose jobs have disappeared. They are additions to the workforce. The total impact on average cost per student is surely significant, albeit difficult to measure accurately. It is an impact felt today that was not felt in 1980. Unfortunately, in contrast to the experience in other service industries, this addition to costs appears to be mostly a net addition, as offsetting cost savings have been relatively modest thus far.

Indeed, it has long been argued that higher education is destined to become relatively more expensive over the long run because higher education is not able to achieve productivity gains comparable to the gains achieved by the economy as a whole. The premise, in other words, is that input-output relationships are relatively more stagnant in higher education than in many other industries. Baumol and Blackman (1995) provide a thoughtful discussion of this issue.

A decrease in instructional workload per faculty, a key input-output relationship, may have led to higher average instructional costs per student in the first few decades after World War II, in conjunction with the growth in university-based research (James, 1978). However, in examining the period from 1972 to 1992, Milam, Berger, and Dey (2000) found that any drift away from time spent on teaching has apparently stopped, as faculty report spending more time on both teaching and research in various types of four-year institutions. The authors speculate that faculty may be spending less time on advising. Apart from overall trends, individual institutions can always change the student-faculty ratio either upward to gain efficiency or downward to enhance their reputation for quality, with a corresponding impact on average costs.

While the discussion thus far has focused mostly on the direct costs of instruction, the indirect costs—those associated with the activities and services that support instruction—need to be attended to as well. It appears that changes in average support costs per student are at least partly responsible for the recent increase in the average full cost (direct plus indirect) per student. For the period examined by Harter, Wade, and Watkins (2005), the share of expenditures spent on instruction declined relative to some support areas. For the years from 2000 to 2003, Middaugh (2005) found that instructional expenditures per credit hour increased, but at a rate less than that of general price inflation. Gumport and Pusser (1995), Leslie and Rhoades (1995), and Morphew and Baker (2004) explore reasons that administrative costs increase.

The number of students enrolled is typically treated as a measure of instructional output (in the absence of measures of learning). From another equally viable perspective, students are an input. The quality of that input has an impact on costs. For example, the total cost of instruction at the typical community college would be different if all of its students were prepared for college work and did not need remediation or developmental instruction in large numbers. On the other end of the student continuum, the most highly sought after students have high expectations and can shop around. Satisfying their demands can lead institutions into a costly race in which facilities and services are added and embellished more from a desire to compete for those students than an inherent need to provide additional support for the educational process.

The impact of outputs on average costs per student can take two forms: a change in either the quantity or the mix of outputs. Both changes can be conceptualized as movements along the average cost curve.

Marginal costs could be greater than average costs for institutions operating near capacity, making additional growth relatively expensive. The converse could also be true. Loss of enrollment would drive up costs if marginal savings were less than average costs, which would be the case if an institution finds it difficult to shed resources in proportion to declines in enrollment.

If student demand shifts from low-cost to high-cost programs, average cost per student will increase absent changes in the respective production functions. The low-cost versus high-cost dimension could be horizontal in the sense of movement among disciplines at the same level of instruction, or vertical in the sense of a shift in the proportion of enrollment by level of instruction rather than among disciplines. Either one or both could have an impact on average cost. This possibility underscores the need to be careful when characterizing an institution's instructional output.

Conclusion

Higher education operating costs will be an important issue for the foreseeable future. Thoughtful analysis is critical to support policymakers in dealing with those costs. Institutional researchers are well positioned to provide that support. To that end, they can learn much about the behavior of costs in higher education by internalizing the economic model of costs as an explanatory paradigm, examining higher education cost studies undertaken by econometricians for empirical findings and methodologies, and employing the tools of economists to identify, compare, and interpret costs in their own local situation. Those concepts, findings, and methods address important questions: What happens to unit costs when output changes? Can some outputs be produced less expensively when produced jointly rather than separately? What factors influence costs? How do average and marginal costs behave in theory and in practice? Generally what are the possibilities for greater efficiency in the production of instruction and research? Some of the questions may never be answered definitively, but economics continues to contribute to a growing body of knowledge about costs—one that is of value for institutional researchers in their roles as information providers and policy analysts.

References

Allen, R. H., and Brinkman, P. T. *Marginal Costing Techniques for Higher Education.* Boulder, Colo.: National Center for Higher Education Management Systems, 1983.

Baumol, W., and Blackman, S. A. B. "How to Think About Rising College Costs." *Planning for Higher Education,* 1995, 23(4), 1–7.

Bowen, H. R. *The Cost of Higher Education: How Much Do Colleges and Universities Spend per Student and How Much Should They Spend?* San Francisco: Jossey-Bass, 1980.

Brinkman, P. T. "Simultaneous Equation Bias in Higher Education Cost Functions." *Research in Higher Education,* 1985, 23(2), 201–218.

Brinkman, P. T. "Higher Education Cost Functions." In S. A. Hoenack and E. L. Collins (eds.), *The Economics of American Universities.* Albany: State University of New York Press, 1990.

Brinkman, P. T. "Factors That Influence Costs in Higher Education." In C. S. Hollins (ed.), *Containing Costs and Improving Productivity in Higher Education.* New Directions for Institutional Research, no. 75. San Francisco: Jossey-Bass, 1992.

Brinkman, P. T., and Allen, R. H. "Concepts of Cost and Cost Analysis for Higher Education." *AIR Professional File,* 1986, 23, 1–8.

Brinkman, P. T., and Leslie, L. L. "Economies of Scale in Higher Education: Sixty Years of Research." *Review of Higher Education,* 1986, 10, 1–28.

Clotfelter, C. T. *Buying the Best: Cost Escalation in Elite Higher Education.* Princeton, N.J.: Princeton University Press, 1996.

Dundar H., and Lewis, D. R. "Departmental Productivity in American Universities: Economies of Scale and Scope." *Economics of Education Review,* 1995, 14(2), 119–144.

Ehrenberg, R. G. *Tuition Rising: Why College Costs So Much.* Cambridge, Mass.: Harvard University Press, 2000.

Getz, M., and Siegfried, J. J. "Costs and Enrollment." In C. T. Clotfelter, R. Ehrenberg, M. Getz, and J. J. Siegfried (eds.), *Economic Challenges in Higher Education.* Chicago: University of Chicago Press, 1991.

Gumport, P. J., and Pusser, B. "A Case of Bureaucratic Accretion: Context and Consequences." *Journal of Higher Education,* 1995, *66*(5), 493–520.

Harter, J.F.R., Wade, J. A., and Watkins, T. G. "An Examination of Costs at Four-Year Public Colleges and Universities Between 1989 and 1998." *Review of Higher Education,* 2005, *28*(3), 369–392.

Hoenack, S. A. "An Economist's Perspective on Costs Within Higher Education Institutions." In S. A. Hoenack and E. L. Collins (eds.), *The Economics of American Universities.* Albany: State University of New York Press, 1990.

Hyatt, J. *A Cost Accounting Handbook.* Washington, D.C.: National Association of College and University Business Officers, 1983.

James, E. "Product Mix and Cost Disaggregation: A Reinterpretation of the Economics of Higher Education." *Journal of Human Resources,* 1978, *13,* 157–186.

Johnes, J., and Johnes, G. "Research Funding and Performance in U.K. University Departments of Economics: A Frontier Analysis." *Economics of Education Review,* 1995, *14,* 301–314.

Layzell, D. T., and Caruthers, J. K. "Higher Education Costs: Concepts, Measurement Issues, Data Sources, and Uses." *Planning for Higher Education,* 2002, *30*(3), 6–14.

Leslie, L. L., and Rhoades, G. "Rising Administrative Costs: Seeking Explanations." *Journal of Higher Education,* 1995, *66*(2), 187–212.

Middaugh, M. F. "Faculty Productivity: Different Strategies for Different Audiences." *Planning for Higher Education,* 2002, *30*(3), 34–43.

Middaugh, M. F. "Understanding Higher Education Costs." *Planning for Higher Education,* 2005, *33*(3), 5–18.

Milam, J. F., Berger, J. B., and Dey, E. L. "Faculty Time Allocation: A Study of Change over Twenty Years." *Journal of Higher Education,* 2000, *71*(4), 454–475.

Morphew, C. C., and Baker, B. D. "The Cost of Prestige: Do New Research I Universities Incur Higher Administrative Costs?" *Review of Higher Education,* 2004, *27*(3), 365–384.

National Commission on the Cost of Higher Education. *Straight Talk About College Costs and Prices.* Phoenix, Ariz.: Oryx Press, 1998.

Rooney, P. M., Borden, V. M. H., and Thomas, T. J. "How Much Does Instruction and Research Really Cost?" *Planning for Higher Education,* 1997, *27*(3), 42–54.

Simpson, W. A., and Sperber, W. E. "A New Type of Cost Analysis for Planners in Academic Departments." *Planning for Higher Education,* 1984, *12*(3), 13–17.

Toutkoushian, R. K. "The Value of Cost Functions for Policymaking and Institutional Research." *Research in Higher Education,* 1999, *40*(1), 1–15.

PAUL T. BRINKMAN *is associate vice president for budget and planning at the University of Utah.*

4

This chapter demonstrates how institutional researchers at institutions of higher education can use economic theory for enrollment management.

Using Economic Concepts to Inform Enrollment Management

Stephen L. DesJardins, Allison Bell

In its simplest and earliest form, enrollment management was the gatekeeping function of an institution, overseen largely by the admissions office (Hossler, 1996). For much of its history, enrollment management has been focused on admitting the appropriate number of students and offering them sufficient amounts of financial aid so that an institution's first choice of students will enroll as freshmen (Coomes, 2000). In its current state, enrollment management focuses on many things besides recruitment and the packaging of financial aid. The scope of enrollment management includes trying to increase the pool of prospective students, attracting applicants, optimizing financial aid packages, establishing effective student services, and trying to maximize the chances that students will successfully complete their academic careers (Hossler, 2000).

The support that institutional researchers provide to the enrollment management functions of their institutions is highly valuable. As institutions of higher education (IHEs) compete for financial resources, administrators are relying more heavily on institutional researchers to explain and predict why students decide to apply to, enroll, and continue to graduation in an institution. Institutional researchers are also key support personnel in determining how institutions can allocate their resources more efficiently and effectively, and much of this type of work has an enrollment management aspect.

We believe enrollment management efforts can be informed by economic concepts, and in this chapter we provide information about foundational

NEW DIRECTIONS FOR INSTITUTIONAL RESEARCH, no. 132, Winter 2006 © Wiley Periodicals, Inc.
Published online in Wiley InterScience (www.interscience.wiley.com) • DOI: 10.1002/ir.196

59

economic concepts that can be used to assist enrollment management decision making. Where appropriate, we provide examples or citations to research that may help institutional researchers use an economic lens from which to view enrollment management issues. (For a more general treatment of the economics of higher education, see Becker and Lewis, 1982.)

Underlying much of microeconomic theory is the idea that individuals are actors in a variety of markets and make decisions that will maximize their well-being. Much of economic theory is based on how individuals act in consumer markets, but this idea of individualism may also hold true for many other decisions that people make, including how much to invest in their own education. Regarding the latter, economists use the theory of human capital to explain how individuals make decisions regarding the amount of education to acquire. Human capital can be thought of as the collective skills and attributes that enable individuals to become more productive in the workplace, thereby leading to higher salaries, and this connection is often referred to by economists as an "investment in human capital" (see Becker, 1964, for details).

Human capital theory is important for enrollment management because it can provide a conceptual basis for student and institutional decision making. Students identify the different educational choices that are feasible for them, and they weigh the benefits (higher future incomes, nonpecuniary factors) and costs (forgone earnings, tuition and fees) of these alternatives (see DesJardins and Toutkoushian, 2005, for additional details). This framework has been the conceptual basis for many studies of student behavior, including the student choice and student demand literature (Jackson and Weathersby, 1975; Kohn, Manski, and Mundel, 1976; Chapman, 1979; Venti and Wise, 1982; Weiler, 1984, 1987; Hossler, Braxton, and Coopersmith, 1989; Paulsen, 1990; Kane, 1994; DesJardins, Dundar, and Hendel, 1999; Hossler, Schmit, and Vesper, 1999; St. John, Asker, and Hu, 2001; Toutkoushian, 2001; DesJardins, Ahlburg, and McCall, 2006).

Embedded in human capital theory is the notion that individuals are rational actors and attempt to maximize their well-being, or "utility." Many economic models posit that individuals make many decisions, including college attendance decisions, based on the utility derived from different schooling options, and not simply based on the net financial benefits. The utility framework takes into account not only the perceived financial net benefits, but also nonpecuniary benefits and costs of each choice and the satisfaction students derive from these choices. Although a student's utility is strictly unobservable, we can infer utility maximization by observing students' choices and statistically model observed actions as a proxy. This framework provides the theoretical basis for probability models estimating student choice on whether to go to college, where to apply, and, conditional on admission, whether to enroll (see DesJardins, Ahlburg, and McCall, 2006, for an example). An important factor that enters into the utility calculations of individuals is the return they can expect from investing in a college education. While both private and social rates of return are important when it comes to considering education, here we focus on the individual or private rates only. A traditional economic perspective predicts that the decision to invest in higher education is influenced by expected costs and benefits, financial resources, academic ability, perceived labor market opportunities, personal preferences and tastes, and uncertainty (Becker, 1964).

The utility maximization framework can also be applied to other decision-making units, such as IHEs. For instance, the decisions institutions make about admitting students parallels the individual decision-making structure discussed above. Institutions often base admission on the ACT or SAT tests and high school performance of students. This strategy is often designed to enroll a class that will generate sufficient tuition revenues, achieve a level of diversity in keeping with the IHE's mission, and attract students whose academic potential is congruent with faculty expectations. Thus, like individual students, institutions also have utility functions comprising varying objectives depending on the mission and goals of the institution.

Economics can help us better understand the behavior of individuals and IHEs alike, but it is the aggregation of these actors and their actions that comprises the educational market. In order to successfully apply economic concepts to enrollment management issues, it is also important to have an understanding of the foundational market concepts of supply and demand.

Demand refers to the quantity of a good that consumers are willing and able to buy at a given price, whereas *supply* depicts the relationship between the quantity of a good that producers are willing and able to supply at a given price. In the realm of enrollment management, the good supplied is the education offered by IHEs, the consumers are students and their families, the producers are the institutions, and the price is the tuition charged in a given semester or academic year. One of the main functions of enrollment managers is to craft a class that is large enough to generate revenues sufficient to operate the educational enterprise. However, attracting students is difficult, as they have many higher education options. Whether students apply to a college, where they eventually decide to matriculate, and whether IHEs have the capacity or desire to admit these students is a function of many of the factors that influence the demand and supply of other consumer products. The factors that influence how much consumers (such as students and their families) are willing and able to purchase (in other words, the quantity demanded or Q_{xD} in equation 4.1 below) are the price of the good in question (tuition, or P_x); the income levels of students and their families, represented by Y; the prices of complementary ($such as room and board, books) and substitute goods and services (such as tuition levels at other IHEs), represented by P_c and P_s; the expected price of the good in future periods ($P_{x,\,t+1}^e$); and the tastes and preferences of consumers, represented by TP (Hirshleifer, 1980; Maurice and Smithson, 1985). This relationship can be represented by

$$Q_{xD} = f(P_x, Y, P_c, P_s, P_{x,\,t+1}^e, TP).\qquad(4.1)$$

Knowing the determinants of demand can help institutional researchers identify important elements that might affect how students make college choice and continuation decisions. For a formal treatment of the demand for higher education, see Becker (1990), and for one that includes issues of enrollment forecasting, see Hoenack and Weiler (1979).

The quantity demanded for a particular good (including college attendance) is affected by each of the terms on the right-hand side of equation 4.1. The first law of demand indicates that as the price of a good increases (decreases), the quantity demanded will fall (rise), ceteris paribus (other things held constant). Given the negative relationship between price and quantity demanded, the typical demand curve is downward sloping (see Figure 4.1), reflecting that prices must be reduced in order to increase quantity demanded.

An important distinction to make is the difference between price-induced changes in quantity demanded versus changes or shifts in demand that occur because of changes in the nonprice determinants of demand. Price-induced changes in quantity demanded result in movements along the demand curve (see Figure 4.1). If enrollment demand at your IHE is represented by D_1 and the tuition (price) increases from p_0 to p_1, enrollments (quantity demanded) will decline from q_0 to q_1. The price-induced change is indicated by the movement from the price/quantity pair at point a to a

**Figure 4.1. Changes in Quantity Demanded Versus Changes
or Shifts in Demand**

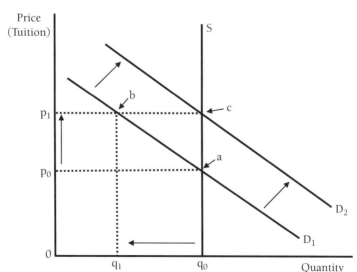

new price/quantity combination at b. A common mistake is to describe this as a change in demand, but changes in demand are due to changes in one or more of the nonprice factors included in equation 4.1. For instance, ceteris paribus, if incomes rise among our prospective students, we might expect the enrollment demand for our IHE to increase, as depicted in Figure 4.1 by an income-induced shift in demand from D_1 to D_2. And if incomes decline, the reverse would be the case.

The example provided in Figure 4.1 demonstrates how an observed increase in price could be due to movement along a fixed demand curve (from point a to point b) or a change or shift in demand (from D_1 to D_2) that results in a new equilibrium price at point c. This example assumes that income changes induce a shift in demand, but other nonprice factors in equation 4.1 can also cause changes or shifts in demand. (For information about how changes in these additional determinants of demand affect the position of the demand curve, see Hirshleifer, 1980, or any microeconomics text.)

Elasticity

How sensitive quantity demanded is to changes in price is measured by a ratio known as the price elasticity of demand. This ratio,

$$E_p = \frac{\%\Delta Qx}{\%\Delta Px} < 0, \tag{4.2}$$

indicates how the percentage change (denoted by $\%\Delta$) in the quantity demanded will change given a percentage change in the price of X. Those with a calculus background will note that the relationship presented in equation 4.2 could also be represented in derivative form by $\partial Qx/\partial Px < 0$ where ∂ indicates the partial effect. This ratio can help us understand the magnitude of changes in enrollment when tuition (price) changes. The ratio of proportionate changes is used to avoid the difficulty that different units of measurement in the numerator and denominator may induce, and having a quantity that is not affected by the units of measurement also facilitates elasticity comparisons for different groups of students (in-state versus nonresidents), by institutional type (four-year versus two-year institutions), or differences over time.

Elasticities greater than one (in absolute value) indicate that the percentage change in quantity demanded is greater than the percentage change in price. If the absolute value of the price elasticity is less than one, then the percentage change in quantity demanded is less than the percentage change in price. When demand is linear, the midpoint of the function is where the percentage change in quantity demanded is equal to the percentage change in price (unitary elasticity of demand; see Figure 4.2). Between the unitary point and the price (quantity) axis is the elastic (inelastic) region. Price, quantity, and total revenue relationships are different in the elastic and inelastic portions of the demand curve. Figure 4.2 can also be used to visualize the

Figure 4.2. Elasticity and Revenue Relationships

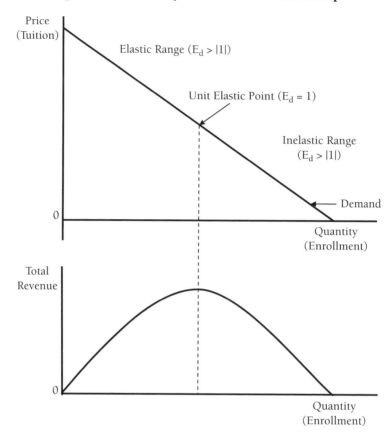

direction of total revenue changes when prices rise or fall in the elastic and inelastic regions of the demand curve (more on total revenue below).

For example, suppose you determine that your institution's price (tuition) elasticity of demand (enrollment) is −.55 (inelastic). You verify this estimate is reasonable by examining the literature on tuition responsiveness (Leslie and Brinkman, 1987; Heller, 1997). Assume your IHE wants to raise tuition by 10 percent and wants you to provide an estimate of the effect that this change will have on enrollments. This is easy to determine by applying equation 4.2:

$$-0.55 = \frac{\%\Delta Qx}{10\%}$$

Rearranging terms:

$$\%\Delta Q = -0.55 * 10\%$$
$$\%\Delta Q = -5.5\%.$$

Figure 4.3. Total Revenue Changes Given Price Changes in Elastic and Inelastic Ranges

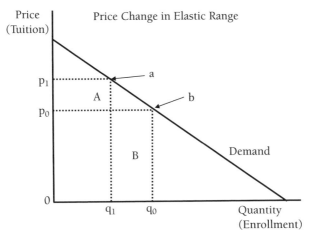

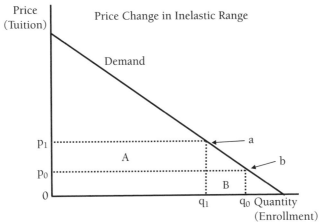

You inform the provost that a 10 percent increase in tuition (price) is likely to result in a reduction in enrollments (quantity demanded) of about 5.5 percent (ceteris paribus). Knowledge of tuition elasticity is also crucial to understanding how total revenue (price times quantity) is affected by tuition changes. Figure 4.3 (top panel) displays what happens to total revenue when the price (tuition) rises from p_0 to p_1 in the elastic portion of the demand curve. When price is p_0, total revenue is bounded by $0p_0bq_0$ and when the price rises to p_1, total revenue is equal to the rectangle bounded by $0p_1aq_1$. The price rise increases total revenues by the rectangle represented by A; however, the price increase also induces a reduction in the quantity demanded, resulting in a total revenue decline of B (because quantity demanded declined from q_0 to q_1). Because A < B, the net total revenue declines due to the price rise. The general relationship is that price changes and total revenue are inversely related when operating in the elastic portion of the demand curve. The converse is true when operating in the inelastic range of the demand curve (see the bottom panel). On balance, A > B implying that total revenue increases due to the price increase.

Elasticity measures are also available for the other determinants of demand, and an important one for enrollment managers to understand is the income elasticity of demand. This ratio measures the relative responsiveness of quantity demanded to changes in income, holding other things in the demand equation constant. This relationship can be represented by

$$E_Y = \frac{\%\Delta Qx}{\%\Delta Y} \qquad (4.3)$$

where E_Y is the income elasticity of demand, Y is a measure of income, and the numerator is quantity demanded. A positive sign on E_Y indicates a "normal" good, meaning that increases (decreases) in income result in increases (decreases) in quantity demanded. A negative sign indicates an "inferior" good, meaning that increases (decreases) in income result in decreases (increases) in quantity demanded.

Enrollments in higher education are typically thought of as a normal good, and estimates of income elasticity are typically slightly inelastic (slightly greater than 1.0), meaning that for each 1 percent increase (decrease) in income, enrollments increase (decrease) by about 1 percent.

If an increase in the price of one good induces an increase in the quantity demanded of another good, these goods are said to be *substitutes*. Examples of substitutes are using part-time faculty rather than full-time faculty or individuals attending college rather than entering the labor force. Goods are *complements* if an increase in the price of either will cause a decrease in the quantity demanded of both goods. A measure used to judge whether goods are substitutes or complements is the cross-price elasticity of demand. It measures the relative responsiveness of the quantity demanded for good X when the price of good Y changes (ceteris paribus), and is represented by

$$E_{XY} = \frac{\%\Delta Qx}{\%\Delta PY} \qquad (4.4)$$

where the numerator is the quantity demanded of good X (such as part-time faculty) and P_Y is the price of good Y (salaries of full-time faculty). The sign of the cross-price elasticity is positive (negative) when X and Y are substitutes (complements). Heller (1999) found positive cross-price responses between four-year comprehensive IHEs and community colleges, indicating they are substitutes. Thus, when the former increase tuition, enrollments increase in the latter. As an example of a nonprice cross-elasticity, if the University of Illinois increases its admissions standards, it may induce increased enrollments at competing institutions such as the University of Iowa or Indiana University.

Consumers' tastes and preferences also affect the demand for goods and services, but the direction of their effects is not determinable a priori. IHEs spend considerable resources to shape prospective students' tastes and preferences, and this is done by enrollment managers within the institution or by hiring enrollment management consultants and marketing firms. These efforts often entail direct mail marketing and telemarketing campaigns (see DesJardins, 2002, for details on using inferential analysis to enhance institutional marketing efforts), policies to encourage campus visits, and advertising campaigns. One objective of these efforts is to change students' propensities of application and enrollment.

Supply-Side Considerations

The amount producers are willing to supply is related to the price they can garner for the good, plus a number of other factors (Maurice and Smithson, 1985). Besides price (P_x), the other factors that affect the amount supplied in a given time period are the state of technology (for example, innovations in teaching delivery such as distance education, represented by T), the price (P_x) and changes in price of inputs (F; labor costs, the largest in higher education, land, and capital), the price of substitute and complementary goods, and expectations about future prices of the good ($P^e_{x,\,t+1}$) (Maurice and Smithson, 1985). The factors affecting supply can be represented by

$$Q_{xS} = f(P_x, F, P_c, P_s, P^e_{x,\,t+1}, T).$$
(4.5)

The slope of the typical supply curve is positive, indicating that firms must be induced by higher prices to produce additional goods and services. Thus, price elasticity of supply is positive and can be used to measure how sensitive supply is to changes in price. There are, of course, nonprice supply elasticities that parallel the demand side elasticities. We leave it up to the reader to investigate these in any microeconomics textbook.

$$E_S = \frac{\%\Delta Qx}{\%\Delta Px} > 0.$$
(4.6)

The typical microeconomic model in which supply and demand interact to clear the market and determine equilibrium price may not hold for the higher education industry, especially on the supply side. For instance, many IHEs are unwilling or unable (at least in the short run) to supply seats to students even if the students are willing to pay increasingly higher prices. Thus, the elasticity of the supply function may be very different depending on the IHE's degree of selectivity. Clotfelter (1991) notes that differences in

Figure 4.4. Application Supply in Open Admissions Versus Selective Institutions

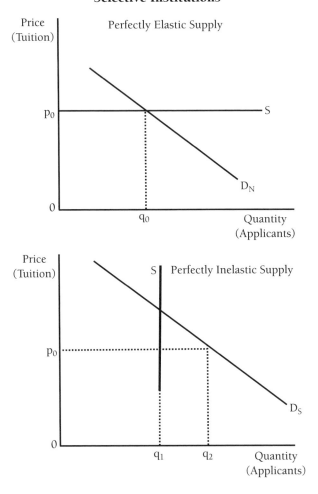

application policies at two hypothetical IHEs can be analyzed using standard economic theory, even when the market clearing treatment does not apply (see Figure 4.4).

For the sake of expository simplicity, assume tuition (price) is constant (p_0) at two institutions: one that is open admissions and the other that is selective in admissions. The nonselective IHE's situation is represented by the graph on the top, where demand for admission is D_N and the number of applicants accepted is determined by the intersection of the demand and horizontal (perfectly elastic) supply curve.

The number of applicants at the prevailing tuition is q_0. Under this admissions policy, the institution will accept all students, so enrollment is determined by demand for seats at this IHE. In contrast, the selective institution constrains supply at q_1, as represented by the perfectly inelastic (vertical) supply curve. At the prevailing tuition level, q_2, applicants are seeking admission; thus, there is excess demand in the amount of $q_2 - q_1$. This demonstrates how it is possible for the supply of places at an institution to determine enrollment levels.

Supply-side considerations also have implications for how enrollments are estimated. For instance, Weiler (1987) notes that studies of enrollment demand "typically assume that public institutions accept all eligible applicants," but "if enrollments are limited by institutional constraints on the supply of places, another approach to estimating student demand behavior is needed" (p. 51). Weiler demonstrates how to conduct such analyses under different assumptions about the supply side. These examples demonstrate how important a sound understanding of the supply side of an IHE is for enrollment management research and practice.

Price Discrimination

Price discrimination is the practice of charging different prices to different consumers for the same good or charging consumers different prices based on the quantity purchased. Perfect price discrimination is charging individual consumers an amount equal to their willingness to pay. Second-degree price discrimination is when the price per unit depends on the amount of the good bought. Third-degree price discrimination is the practice of dividing the relevant market into groups (segments) based on their price elasticities and charging each of these segments different prices for the same good. Due to limitations in determining each individual's price elasticity, engaging in first-degree price discrimination is often very difficult, and second-degree pricing does not make much sense for IHEs. However, institutions often engage in third-degree price discrimination by segmenting their market and then charging different tuition for these segments (such as residents versus nonresidents, graduate versus undergraduate students, and upper- versus lower-division students). Institutions try to discern the tuition responsiveness of students using information from the testing agencies (ACT and SAT) and from the Free Application for Student Assistance (see DesJardins, 1999, 2002, or Toutkoushian, 2001, for examples).

In one of the earliest studies of differential pricing, Berg and Hoenack (1987) examined the feasibility and effects of charging upper-division students higher tuition than their lower-division (freshman and sophomore) counterparts. Their main rationale for differential pricing was that students have different sensitivities to tuition because it is costly for students to transfer to another IHE, these costs typically rise as students become more invested in an institution, and as their academic careers progress, there may be fewer close substitutes. These reasons suggest that upper-division students' tuition elasticities of enrollment are likely to be less sensitive to tuition increases (more inelastic) than their lower division peers. Also, if upper-division students' tuition elasticity is less than 1, tuition increases targeted toward them will result in increased tuition revenue (ceteris paribus).

Another way institutions engage in price discrimination is by practicing tuition discounting, which is providing "institutionally funded grant aid to help defray students' college expenses" with the objective of influencing their enrollment decision (Davis, 2003, p. 3). The ability of institutions to use tuition discounting varies widely by institution type and available resources (such as endowments); however, all institutions subsidize at least a portion of the cost of educating students (Winston, 1999). These subsidies are designed to lower the cost of higher education to students by reducing their net price, defined as the "sticker," or posted, tuition less any institutional grants or scholarships. Tuition discounting has become an increasingly popular way to attract students (Lapovsky and Hubbell, 2003). For example, in the mid-1990s, the University of Iowa experienced continuing declines in enrollments of nonresident students largely because many of its competitors had been discounting to prospective students. Thus, Iowa found itself in a situation where failure to respond to competitive pressures would likely result in continued erosion of nonresident enrollments and the substantial tuition revenue they generated. Administrators decided to offer a new scholarship to selected nonresident students, in effect, discounting the Iowa sticker price to nonresident students. DesJardins (2001a, 2001b) demonstrated how the effects of this policy proposal were estimated and simulated using many of the economic concepts discussed above: not only could this discounting strategy increase enrollments from the targeted group, but net tuition revenue could also be increased.

Subsidies from noninstitutional sources (federal and state government, private sources) also reduce the net price of attendance for students. Many different types of financial aid are provided to students, and the effect of these subsidies on enrollment (Hossler, 2000) and graduation (DesJardins, Ahlburg, and McCall, 2002) has been heavily studied. These subsidies, whether from an IHE's coffers or not, can often remedy some of the differentials in elasticities among prospective students. For instance, research has shown that financial aid offers to low-income students may ameliorate some of the enrollment probability differences relative to their higher-income counterparts (McPherson and Schapiro, 1989; St. John, 1990; Heller, 1997). McPherson and Schapiro (1998) also provide an excellent treatment of how financial aid is used as a competitive weapon and offer an interesting discussion of merit aid from the institutions' and students' perspective.

Finally, institutional researchers can conduct analyses of enrollments using both price and financial aid elasticity concepts. DesJardins (1999) examined the effects of a proposal to increase the tuition of Wisconsin students attending the University of Minnesota. Using information about the tuition and aid elasticities of these students, he created three financial aid need groups and estimated enrollment changes for each segment. Given limited time to conduct this study, the elasticities for each of these three groups were obtained from the existing literature (St. John, 1990, 1994). A simple spreadsheet was constructed that allowed the analyst to report (in real time) to a group of decision makers the likely enrollment impact of the proposed tuition surcharge. The analysis revealed that enrollments would decline insignificantly, yet net tuition revenue would increase by almost $200,000. These results confirmed what the author suspected a priori: Wisconsin students' sensitivity to tuition changes was relatively inelastic.

Conclusion

The primary goal of this chapter was to provide institutional researchers with an understanding of simple yet powerful economic concepts that, when properly applied, can inform enrollment management research and institutional decision making. A foundational understanding of supply and demand and how they interact to determine prices is necessary (but not sufficient) if institutional researchers are to understand the educational marketplace in which their institutions operate. Institutional research professionals should also have a firm understanding of related concepts such as elasticity, in particular, price (tuition) elasticity of demand (enrollment), because of its utility in estimating tuition revenue when tuition levels change. Also, as DesJardins (2001a, 2001b) demonstrated, price elasticity concepts can be used to estimate enrollment levels under various tuition (pricing) scenarios using basic inferential methods and common spreadsheet software.

Although there are untold situations where simple economic principles can inform enrollment management efforts, many factors may complicate these applications. Weiler (1987) demonstrated how deviations from classical supply-side assumptions may affect how institutional researchers estimate enrollment levels at their institutions. This is a demonstration of how real-world situations can and do complicate the analysis that institutional researchers conduct and how a solid understanding of economic principles can assist in thinking through such complications. Our suggestion is that if you confront a situation in which you are unsure of how economic theory can be applied, look to the literature. There are many articles and books available in the economics and higher education literature where researchers have used economic theory as the conceptual basis of projects that have institutional research and enrollment management implications. Although they may not map to a specific issue or problem, many times they provide the guidance needed as the foundation for a study. For example, DesJardins' 1999 study of the enrollment and tuition revenue effects of changes to the tuition reciprocity agreement between Minnesota and Wisconsin could not have been completed in time to affect the decision-making process had he not obtained important information on tuition and aid elasticities from an article published in 1994 by St. John.

In conjunction with the other chapters presented in this volume, we hope the conceptual information presented here, and its application to enrollment management issues, has been instructive. It is our sincere hope that our efforts will assist institutional researchers in being even more effective in the conduct of enrollment management research at their institutions of higher education.

References

Becker, G. *Human Capital: A Theoretical and Empirical Analysis with Special Reference to Education.* Cambridge, Mass.: National Bureau of Economic Research, 1964.

Becker, W. "The Demand for Higher Education." In S. A. Hoenack and E. L. Collins (eds.), *The Economics of American Universities.* Albany: State University of New York Press, 1990.

Becker, W., and Lewis, D. *The Economics of American Higher Education.* Norwell, Mass.: Kluwer, 1982.

Berg, D., and Hoenack, S. "The Concept of Cost-Related Tuition and Its Implementation at the University of Minnesota." *Journal of Higher Education,* 1987, *58*(3), 276–305.

Chapman, R. "Pricing Policy and the College Choice Process." *Research in Higher Education,* 1979, *10,* 37–57.

Clotfelter, C. "Explaining the Demand." In C. T. Clotfelter, R. G. Ehrenberg, M. Getz, and J. J. Siegfried (eds.), *Economic Challenges in Higher Education.* Chicago: University of Chicago Press, 1991.

Coomes, M. "The Historical Role of Enrollment Management." In M. Coomes, (ed.), *The Role Student Aid Plays in Enrollment Management.* New Directions for Student Services, no. 89. San Francisco: Jossey-Bass, 2000.

Davis, J. *Unintended Consequences of Tuition Discounting.* Indianapolis: Lumina Foundation for Education, 2003.

DesJardins, S. "Simulating the Enrollment Effects of Changes in the Tuition Reciprocity Agreement Between Minnesota and Wisconsin." *Research in Higher Education,* 1999, *40*(6), 705–716.

DesJardins, S. "Assessing the Effects of Changing Institutional Aid Policy." *Research in Higher Education,* 2001a, *42*(6), 653–678.

DesJardins, S. "Assessing the Impact of a Change in Institutional Aid Policy: A Simulation Tool." *Journal of Student Financial Aid,* 2001b, *30*(3), 7–16.

DesJardins, S. "An Analytic Strategy to Assist Institutional Recruitment and Marketing Efforts." *Research in Higher Education,* 2002, *43*(5), 531–553.

DesJardins, S., Ahlburg, D., and McCall, B. "Simulating the Longitudinal Effects of Changes in Financial Aid on Student Departure from College." *Journal of Human Resources,* 2002, *37*(3), 653–679.

DesJardins, S., Ahlburg, D., and McCall, B. "An Integrated Model of Application, Admission, Enrollment, and Financial Aid." *Journal of Higher Education,* 2006, *77*(3), 381–429.

DesJardins, S., Dundar, H., and Hendel, D. "Modeling the Application Decision Process at a Land Grant University." *Economics of Education Review,* 1999, *18,* 117–132.

DesJardins, S., and Toutkoushian, R. "Are Students Really Rational? The Development of Rational Thought and Its Application to Student Choice." In J. C. Smart (ed.), *Higher Education: Handbook of Theory and Research.* New York: Springer, 2005.

Heller, D. "Student Price Response in Higher Education: An Update to Leslie and Brinkman." *Journal of Higher Education,* 1997, *68*(6), 624–659.

Heller, D. "The Effects of Tuition and State Financial Aid on Public College Enrollment." *Review of Higher Education,* 1999, *23*(1), 65–89.

Hirshleifer, J. *Price Theory and Applications.* Upper Saddle River, N.J.: Prentice Hall, 1980.

Hoenack, S., and Weiler, W. "The Demand for Higher Education and Institutional Enrollment Forecasting." *Economic Inquiry,* 1979, *17*(1), 89–113.

Hossler, D. "From Admission to Enrollment Management." In A. Rentz (ed.), *Student Affairs Practice in Higher Education.* (2nd ed.) Springfield, Ill.: Charles C. Thomas, 1996.

Hossler, D. "The Role of Financial Aid in Enrollment Management." In M. Coomes, (ed.), *The Role Student Aid Plays in Enrollment Management.* New Directions for Student Services, no. 89. San Francisco: Jossey-Bass, 2000.

Hossler, D., Braxton, J., and Coopersmith, G. "Understanding Student College Choice." In J. C. Smart (ed.), *Higher Education: Handbook of Theory and Research.* New York: Agathon Press, 1989.

Hossler, D., Schmit, J., and Vesper, N. *Going to College: How Social, Economic, and Educational Factors Influence the Decisions Students Make.* Baltimore, Md.: John Hopkins University Press, 1999.

Jackson, G., and Weathersby, G. "Individual Demand for Higher Education." *Journal of Higher Education,* 1975, *46*(6), 623–652.

Kane, T. "College Attendance by Blacks Since 1970: The Role of College Cost, Family Background and the Returns to Education." *Journal of Political Economy,* 1994, *102*(5), 878–911.

Kohn, M., Manski, C., and Mundel, D. "An Empirical Investigation of Factors Which Influence College-Going Behavior." *Annals of Economics and Social Measurement,* 1976, *5*(4), 391–419.

Lapovsky, L., and Hubbell, L. *Tuition Discounting Continues to Grow.* Washington, D.C.: National Association of College and University Business Officers, 2003.

Leslie, L., and Brinkman, P. "Student Price Response in Higher Education." *Journal of Higher Education,* 1987, *58*, 181–204.

Maurice, S., and Smithson, C. *Managerial Economics: Applied Microeconomics for Decision Making.* Homewood, Ill.: Irwin, 1985.

McPherson, M., and Schapiro, M. "Measuring the Effects of Federal Student Aid: An Assessment of Some Methodological and Empirical Problems." Williamstown, Mass.: Williams Project on the Economics of Higher Education, 1989.

McPherson, M., and Schapiro, M. *The Student Aid Game: Meeting Need and Rewarding Talent in American Higher Education.* Princeton, N.J.: Princeton University Press, 1998.

Paulsen, M. *College Choice: Understanding Student Enrollment Behavior.* ASHE-ERIC Higher Education Report, no. 90–6. Washington, D.C.: George Washington University, 1990.

St. John, E. "Price Response in Enrollment Decisions: An Analysis of the High School and Beyond Sophomore Cohort." *Research in Higher Education,* 1990, *31*(2), 161–176.

St. John, E. "Assessing Tuition and Student Aid Strategies: Using Price Response Measures to Simulate Pricing Alternatives." *Research in Higher Education,* 1994, *35*(3), 301–334.

St. John, E., Asker, E., and Hu, S. "The Role of Finances in Student Choice: A Review of Theory and Research." In M. B. Paulsen and J. C. Smart (eds.), *The Finance of Higher Education: Theory, Research, Policy, and Practice.* New York: Agathon Press, 2001.

Toutkoushian, R. "Do Parental Income and Educational Attainment Affect the Initial Choices of New Hampshire's College-Bound Students?" *Economics of Education Review,* 2001, *20*, 245–262.

Venti, S., and Wise, D. "Test Scores, Educational Opportunity, and Individual Choice." *Journal of Public Economics,* 1982, *18*, 35–63.

Weiler, W. "Using Enrollment Demand Models in Institutional Pricing Decisions." In L. Litten (ed.), *Issues in Pricing Undergraduate Education.* San Francisco: Jossey-Bass, 1984.

Weiler, W. "Enrollment Demand with Constrained Supply in a Higher Education Institution." *Research in Higher Education,* 1987, *27*(1), 51–61.

Winston, G. "Subsidies, Hierarchy and Peers: The Awkward Economies of Higher Education." *Journal of Economic Perspectives,* 1999, *13*(1), 13–36.

STEPHEN L. DESJARDINS is associate professor in the Center for the Study of Higher and Postsecondary Education at the University of Michigan.

ALLISON BELL is a doctoral candidate in the Center for the Study of Higher and Postsecondary Education at the University of Michigan.

5

Economic models of the way in which faculty allocate their time, and the behavior of labor markets, can help inform institutional research on faculty in a variety of ways.

Economic Contributions to Institutional Research on Faculty

Robert K. Toutkoushian

A significant part of the work that institutional researchers conduct is related to faculty. Institutional researchers often work directly with the information systems that contain data on their faculty, and thus understand how these data were generated and some of their limitations when reported to various audiences. The fact that many institutional researchers have strong quantitative and methodological skills allows them to understand the different implications of using data on faculty for decision making. For these reasons, institutional researchers increasingly act as mediators between the producers and the users of faculty data.

To do this effectively, institutional researchers need to understand the theoretical frameworks behind the activities of faculty. Economics can play a significant role in this regard. Economists strive to model how decision makers behave in particular markets. The models rely on the premise that decision makers are trying to achieve specific goals, such as maximizing utility, while working with limited resources. This approach can be applied to faculty, who have to make decisions about how to allocate their time between competing activities, and institutions, which must employ full-time faculty and other inputs to achieve educational goals. Economists then use these models to examine how the equilibrium would change when one or more factors in the model change. This process, known as comparative statics, is perhaps the most valuable use of economics because it provides a way to test hypotheses about the relationships between factors such as gender and faculty salaries. Economists firmly believe that the incentives faced

New Directions for Institutional Research, no. 132, Winter 2006   © Wiley Periodicals, Inc.
Published online in Wiley InterScience (www.interscience.wiley.com) • DOI: 10.1002/ir.197

by decision makers affect their behavior and that policymaking should focus on changing the incentives to elicit changes in behavior. This is certainly applicable to faculty, who often receive substantially greater rewards for research versus teaching and service activities. Similarly, analysts can determine how various policy levers, such as the wage rate for part-time faculty, would affect the use of full-time and part-time faculty by the institution.

In this chapter, I describe how economic theories, models, and reasoning can help shape institutional research work related to faculty. It is not surprising that virtually every study of faculty compensation relies on the foundations of labor markets and economics. Because institutional researchers often produce studies and reports of faculty workload and productivity, the economic theories of individual behavior and time allocation can help them explain to policymakers the implications and limitations of data on faculty. These models have also helped institutional researchers interpret salary and employment statistics on faculty for decision makers on their campuses.

Categories of Institutional Research on Faculty

The work that institutional researchers conduct that is related to faculty can be grouped into four broad categories: (1) external reporting of faculty data for the institution, (2) internal reporting of faculty data for the institution, (3) internal analyses of faculty data for administrators and stakeholders, and (4) scholarly research on issues relating to faculty. Although institutional research has traditionally focused more on the first two aspects, the field is shifting as institutional researchers are increasingly being asked by administrators to provide analyses on faculty issues that will directly inform decision making. Economic theories and reasoning primarily affect the last two areas of institutional research work on faculty, but can also influence the types of data reported to external and internal audiences.

External Reporting on Faculty. Colleges and universities are asked to respond to a variety of requests from external agencies for data and information on their faculty. These requests range from requirements from the federal and state government to report selected statistics on their faculty, to voluntary queries from private enterprises such as professional associations, publications, and the media for faculty information. The information requested may include the numbers of faculty employed, faculty salaries and benefits, and counts of faculty by characteristics such as gender, race/ethnicity, rank, age, and full-time/part-time status. Institutional researchers are frequently charged with the responsibility for responding to these requests. The information is typically used in reports by national and state agencies on education and faculty issues, and as such may be subject to misinterpretation by readers who do not fully understand the underlying issues affecting faculty work and compensation.

Internal Reporting on Faculty. Institutional researchers are also involved in producing reports and tables on their faculty for internal audi-

NEW DIRECTIONS FOR INSTITUTIONAL RESEARCH • DOI: 10.1002/ir

ences at their institution. These audiences may include administrators such as the president, vice presidents, chancellors, deans, and department chairpersons; faculty groups such as academic departments or faculty unions; as well as students and staff. The type of information produced by institutional researchers for these stakeholders includes faculty staffing levels by department, faculty workload statistics on courses taught and research activities, faculty compensation, and teaching evaluations. Often the data are included in a fact book along with data and information on students and institutional finances. For example, Table 5.1 shows hypothetical data on the average salaries by rank for a set of five institutions that use each other as comparators. Statistics such as these require some explanation from institutional researchers. Although Institution A has the highest average faculty salaries within each rank, its overall average salary is lower than for three of its peers due to having a higher concentration of faculty at lower ranks. Likewise, aggregate statistics such as average salaries can mask important factors that can affect comparisons among institutions. For example, the below-average salaries for faculty at Institution F may reflect lower experience levels within ranks or more faculty concentrated in lower-paying fields such as the humanities.

In addition, there are significant limitations to the type of information that can be obtained on faculty activities. Ideally a comprehensive analysis of faculty work activities and compensation would include both the inputs into teaching, research, and service and the outputs from these activities. Unfortunately, the data rarely exist on all inputs, and measuring outputs even in research and service can be elusive. Table 5.2 provides a list of faculty work activities broken down by availability to institutional researchers.

Internal Analyses of Faculty. Increasingly, institutional researchers are being asked not only to provide data on faculty to internal and external audiences but also to interpret and analyze data for use in decision making at the institution. In this way, institutional researchers are being seen less as the keepers of data on faculty and more as the group that can explain what the data on faculty mean for policymaking. These may be presented in the form of studies of a particular issue or the development of performance indicators for the institution. Following are examples of the types of questions posed to institutional researchers by administrators and other stakeholders:

- Is the institution competitive with other institutions in terms of faculty compensation?
- Is the balance between faculty at different ranks changing, and if so, what are the implications for the institution?
- How many faculty members are likely to retire in the coming years, and how will this affect the institution?
- How should the institution evaluate the work activities and accomplishments of its faculty?

Table 5.1. Hypothetical Report on Average Faculty Salaries by Rank for Seven Institutions

Institution	Full Professors		Associate Professors		Assistant Professors		All Faculty	
	Salary	Number	Salary	Number	Salary	Number	Salary	Number
A	$85,000	100	$72,000	160	$55,000	110	$70,459	370
B	$82,000	200	$71,000	180	$55,000	120	$71,560	500
C	$81,000	80	$69,500	50	$53,000	30	$72,156	160
D	$79,500	60	$69,000	40	$52,000	20	$71,417	120
E	$77,500	450	$68,000	300	$52,500	350	$66,955	1100
F	$75,000	150	$67,500	150	$53,000	150	$65,167	450
G	$71,500	120	$65,000	140	$51,000	160	$61,524	420
Totals	**$78,786**		**$68,857**		**$53,071**		**$68,462**	

Table 5.2. Data Availability of Faculty Work Activities

Usually Available	More Difficult to Obtain
• Number of courses taught	• Number and types of committee assignments
• Number of students taught	• Number of scholarly publications
• Amount of money received from research grants	• Quality of scholarly publications
• Summaries from teaching evaluations	• Gains in student learning and achievement
• Scheduled time allocation between teaching, research, and service	• Number of outside service activities
	• Benefits of service activities
	• Benefits from research activities

Institutional researchers are well suited to play this role at their institution. Because they often work closely with the data systems containing information on faculty, they understand the limitations of using these data to address policy questions that administrators raise. Their role in the administrative hierarchy also allows them to learn the reasoning behind requests for analyses and therefore determine how best to respond to these requests. Finally, the fact that many institutional researchers are trained in the use of quantitative methods helps them find the most appropriate format for analyzing and presenting information to decision makers at the institution.

When preparing information and analyses for use in policymaking, the institutional researcher should consider in advance how the information might be used. In many instances, objective information could be used to support different points of view, and some of these uses may create problems for the institution. For example, the report in Table 5.1 showing how the average salaries for faculty at an institution compare to other institutions may be used by the faculty union at Institution G to argue for larger salary increases for faculty and can be used in negotiations of future labor contracts with the administration. Similarly, data showing an increase in student-to-faculty ratios over time may raise concerns about increasing class size and reductions in student learning. Finally, a report showing a difference in average salaries between male and female faculty may lead female faculty at an institution to argue that the administration is engaging in pay discrimination and could eventually lead to legal action against the institution. Virtually any statistic on faculty has the potential to lead to such problems. Although institutional researchers cannot avoid all of these situations when preparing and presenting information, they can inform administrators of these issues in advance by carefully considering the potential impacts and understanding the theoretical framework behind how the data were generated.

In policymaking settings, decisions must often be made with the best available, albeit imperfect, information. Such is certainly the case with regard to institutional policymaking on faculty issues. Institutional researchers who are asked to participate in policymaking must therefore produce data and analyses using the most appropriate information that is available to them. It is common for institutional researchers to produce reports on student-to-faculty ratios and average numbers of courses taught by faculty, despite the fact that these data provide only a partial view of faculty work-related activities. In situations where the information may be used for decision making, it is the role of institutional researchers to alert administrators as to the limitations of the data and what can and cannot be inferred from them.

Scholarly Research on Faculty. The fourth category of work that institutional researchers do in relation to faculty is to conduct research studies on one or more aspects of faculty. These studies can be done using individual, departmental, institutional, regional, or national data depending on the issue at hand. The goal of these studies is to learn more about the processes that affect data on faculty such as their salaries, time allocation, performance, and satisfaction. This type of work is useful because it helps inform the policymaking process described earlier, builds credibility among stakeholders at the institution, provides visibility and recognition to the institutional researcher and his or her office, and provides an external validity check on the work. Unfortunately, this aspect of institutional research is often given less attention than the previous three categories, in part due to the time that may be required to complete the study and the necessary level of quantitative and conceptual skills to conduct the work. Nonetheless, this work has had significant impacts on the profession of institutional research. As institutional researchers become less focused on data management, there will be an even greater demand for those who can analyze data in order to make policy recommendations at their institutions.

Some of the questions that have been addressed through scholarly research on faculty include these:

- How do individual characteristics such as gender, race/ethnicity, age, experience, and educational attainment affect how faculty are paid?
- How do personal and institutional characteristics affect how faculty members allocate their time to teaching, research, and service?
- What could explain the growth in part-time employment among faculty in the United States?
- Will there be enough faculty to meet the demands of students in the future?

All of these questions require more in-depth analysis to answer than can be provided by a single table of figures pulled from an institution's human resource system. Furthermore, the analyses need to be guided by a theoretical framework to help ensure that the results are meaningful and can be justified to multiple stakeholders.

NEW DIRECTIONS FOR INSTITUTIONAL RESEARCH • DOI: 10.1002/ir

Figure 5.1. Time Allocation for an Individual Faculty Member

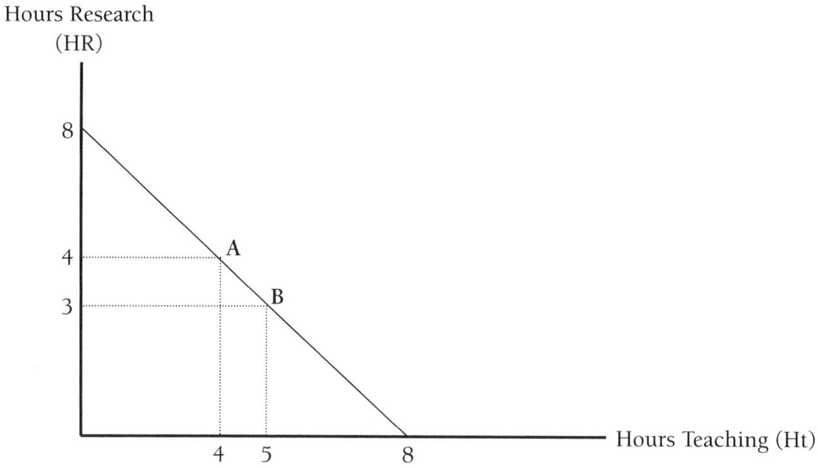

Hours Research
(HR)

Economic Theory of Time Allocation and Productivity

Economics as a field focuses on the allocation of scarce resources among unlimited wants. Although early economic work centered on the allocation of resources such as raw materials and income, Gary Becker (1965) was among the first to articulate that time is also a resource that can be examined through economic reasoning. This insight allowed economic reasoning to be applied to a much wider range of individual and organizational behavior than had been the case prior to this work. Thus, the various aspects of how faculty spend their time and what they produce from these activities can be understood more fully through the economist's lens of individual behavior. Descriptions of the general model of time allocation and utility maximization can be found in almost any intermediate-level textbook, such as Pindyck and Rubinfeld (1989), or selected principles-level textbooks on microeconomics, such as McEachern (1997) and Lieberman and Hall (2000). Researchers who have applied this model directly to the academic labor market include Yuker (1984), Singell, Lillydahl, and Singell (1996), and Bellas and Toutkoushian (1999).

According to this model, all individuals must make decisions about how to allocate their time between competing activities. Because time is a fixed resource, any additional time that is devoted to one activity must come at the expense of another one. This is certainly the case for faculty, who must make decisions about how to divide their time between teaching and all other activities. Figure 5.1 depicts graphically the time constraint faced by a faculty member who, after subtracting time spent in service and nonwork-related activities, has eight hours of discretionary time per day to distribute between teaching and research. Two possible time allocations are highlighted. At point A, the faculty member spends four hours per day teaching and four hours on research, and at point B he or she is spending five hours per day on teaching and three hours per day on research.

The entire time constraint would shift inward as other demands on a faculty member's time increase. Such might be the case if individuals are asked to spend more time serving on department, college, or institutional committees, or family demands for time increase.

Although faculty members are usually obligated to teach a specific number of courses per semester, the actual time that they directly spend on teaching activities (such as preparing for lectures, helping students, and grading) can vary greatly. Economists argue that in making decisions about how to allocate their time, faculty members would estimate the satisfaction, or utility, received from different combinations of teaching and research that fall within their time constraint and choose the combination with the highest level of utility. In a relatively simple model of faculty behavior, an individual's utility could be a function of the income derived from productivity in research (P_r) and teaching (P_t). A Cobb-Douglas production function might be used to describe how time spent in teaching (H_t) and research (H_r) relates to productivity in each area:

$$P_r = H_t^{\alpha 1} H_r^{\alpha 2} \tag{5.1a}$$

$$P_t = H_t^{\beta 1} H_r^{\beta 2} \tag{5.1b}$$

where $\alpha 1$ is the effect of each hour of teaching on research productivity, $\alpha 2$ is the effect of each hour of research on research productivity, $\beta 1$ is the effect of each hour of teaching on teaching productivity, and $\beta 2$ is the effect of each hour of research on teaching productivity. It is reasonable to assume that time spent in each activity has the largest impact on that activity, meaning that the weights attached to each are such that $\alpha 2 > \alpha 1$, $\beta 1 > \beta 2$, $\beta 1 > \alpha 1$, and $\alpha 2 > \beta 2$. The coefficients could be very low, for example, if time spent on teaching has no spillover benefits for research or vice versa.

The Cobb-Douglas functional form gives rise to a production function where total productivity in each area could be higher for combinations of teaching and research than it is when all time is allocated to either extreme. Accordingly, faculty would be most productive overall when they engage in some combination of teaching and research. This is depicted in Figure 5.2.

When considering changes in their time allocation, faculty would compare the benefits of spending more time in one activity, such as teaching, with the costs of doing so. An economist might argue that faculty income (I) is a linear function of their productivity from teaching and research, as in:

Figure 5.2. Production Function for an Individual Faculty Member

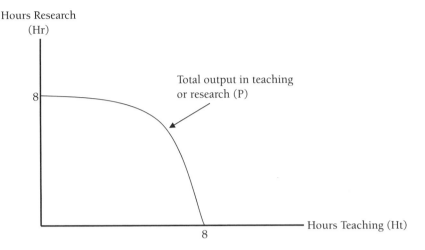

$$I = \gamma_r P_r + \gamma_t P_t \tag{5.2}$$

where γ_r is the reward for research productivity and γ_t is the reward for teaching productivity. The production function framework shows that an increase in time spent in teaching may lead to either gains or losses in overall productivity depending on the magnitude of lost productivity from having to reduce time spent on research, and the extent to which time spent in one activity influences productivity in the other activity (Becker, 1975, 1979, 1982). For example, the additional time that a faculty member spends in research may help improve her productivity in teaching by allowing her to bring new perspectives into the classroom. However, additional time spent in research would take away time spent directly in teaching, and thus the net effect on productivity is ambiguous.

The way in which institutions compensate faculty for different activities would also be predicted to affect their subsequent time allocation between them. At doctoral-granting institutions, and increasingly at master's- and even baccalaureate-level institutions, the reward system for faculty is usually heavily tilted toward research over teaching ($\gamma_r > \gamma_t$). These rewards come in the form of both higher salary and greater likelihood of being promoted and tenured. The high emphasis on research means that the cost of engaging in more teaching to the individual faculty member is higher than the cost of spending more time in research.

It is not surprising, therefore, for stakeholders such as legislators and the general public to raise concerns that faculty are spending less time on teaching than they might think is appropriate. This is important for institutional research because many policymakers have advocated for increasing faculty time spent teaching without considering the costs of such a policy. The time allocation model provides a way of articulating the trade-offs that faculty face when deciding how to spend their time between teaching and research. In addition, the sensitivity of the results from such a model can provide guidance to policymakers interested in changing how faculty members allocate their time. Economists would focus on how changes in the constraints and incentives faced by faculty and the reward structure for faculty could be used to accomplish this. For example, a policy that reduced time spent in service activities would shift the time constraint shown in Figure 5.1 outward, enabling faculty to spend more time on teaching, research, or both. Similarly, increasing the weight given to teaching in promotion and tenure decisions would increase the rewards, and hence utility, of spending more time in teaching.

These models can help inform much of the work that institutional researchers do on faculty. First, because most data reporting mechanisms omit certain aspects of faculty work, institutional researchers understand that misleading inferences regarding work effort and productivity could be drawn from reports and studies that focus on only one particular faculty activity. As institutional researchers are increasingly asked by administrators to help interpret statistics and play a part in policymaking, they are obligated to point out the limitations of such data on faculty.

To illustrate, the Office of Policy Analysis for the University System of New Hampshire was once asked by the board of trustees to prepare information on the teaching activities of faculty at three institutions in the university system (Keene State College, Plymouth State University, and the University of New Hampshire). The primary reason for the request was that several trustees felt that faculty across the system were not teaching enough courses and that the problem was especially bad at the University of New Hampshire. The institutional researchers understood that faculty members are asked to engage in teaching, research, and service activities as part of their job and that the demands for research were greater at the University of New Hampshire than at either Keene State or Plymouth State. A report that focused solely on teaching activities of faculty would therefore understate the amount of work that they perform as part of their jobs, give the misleading impression that faculty at the University of New Hampshire were less productive than their counterparts, and might ignore the opportunity costs and lost productivity that would result if policies were implemented to increase the time that faculty were required to spend on teaching.

Table 5.3 provides some of the information that was compiled by the Office for the Board of Trustees on the teaching activities of faculty. As expected, the results showed that faculty at the University of New Hampshire had fewer credit hours and sections per year than their counterparts at the two other residential campuses. Although staff in the Office of Policy Analysis produced the requested reports, they also took care to explain what board members could and could not infer through the data. For example, the final report cautioned the board that the information provided was not a comprehensive workload analysis of faculty because it omitted many important activities of faculty. The fact that faculty at the University of New Hampshire taught fewer credit hours and courses on average than their counterparts within the university system could be attributed in part to faculty having to spend more time on research activities given the institution's reward structure and emphasis on research. Similarly, this report could not capture other components of instructional time, such as time spent in office hours, grading, and preparing lectures, and does not factor in how the difficulty of the subject matter being taught might affect the time spent on teaching.

Faculty Labor Market

Labor economists posit that workers in any occupation function in a labor market. A labor market can be thought of as a place where buyers of labor (firms) and sellers of labor (people) come together to determine wages and employment levels. In the textbook treatment of labor markets (Borjas, 2000; Ehrenberg and Smith, 2000; McEachern, 1997), economists argue that the demand for any good or service is affected by the price of the good, the demand for the good or services that labor will produce, the price of substitute and competing goods, the demanders' ability to pay for labor, and the number of demanders in the market.

Viewed in this way, the academic labor market is simply a specific kind of labor market where the services of individuals who are qualified to serve as faculty are bought and sold. This is certainly true of the academic labor market, where institutions of higher education are the buyers, or demanders, of faculty labor, and the individuals with the qualifications to be professors are the sellers, or suppliers, or labor. A number of economists have examined the labor market for faculty, including Caplow and McGee (1958), Cartter (1966, 1971,

Table 5.3. Data on Faculty Teaching Activities at University System of New Hampshire Institutions, 1999

Statistic	University of New Hampshire	Keene State College	Plymouth State College
Average number of sections taught per year	4.53	6.71	6.75
Average number of credit hours taught per year	15.83	21.84	21.02
Percentage of enrollments taught by faculty	57	62	62
Percentage of sections taught by faculty	67	61	61

Note: Data are for the 1998–99 academic year and were obtained from the institutional research offices at each institution.

1974), Tuckman (1976), Bowen and Schuster (1986), Breneman and Youn (1988), and Toutkoushian (2003). Applying the labor market model to academia, faculty labor (D_L) will be a function of the wage rate for faculty (w_F), the demand for goods or services produced by faculty in teaching and research (d_t and d_r), the income and wealth of the institution (V_I), the price of substitute resources for faculty (p_s), the price of complementary resources for faculty (p_c), and the number of institutions in the relevant market (N_I). Economists might depict these relationships in the form of an equation such as the following:

$$D_F = f(w_F, d_t, d_r, V_I, p_s, p_c, N_I) \qquad (5.3)$$

This model assumes that holding all else constant, demand for faculty would increase when either the demand for teaching and research services increases, institutional income or wealth increases, the price of substitutes for faculty (such as graduate assistants and adjunct faculty) increases, the price of complements for faculty (such as technology used in the classroom and fringe benefits) decreases, or the number of providers increases. Labor economists describe the demand for labor as a *derived demand,* in that employers demand labor primarily because of the demand for goods and services that labor can produce. In the faculty labor market, this implies that the demand for faculty is derived through the demand for higher education services in teaching (enrollments) and research (grants).

On the supply side of the market, the market supply of a good or service is typically described as a function of the price of the good, the price of other goods that could be made from the firm's resources, the productivity of resources, and the number of suppliers in the market. Continuing with the analogy to education, the market supply curve for faculty (S_F) would be affected by the wage rate for faculty (w_F), the wage rate that faculty could receive in alternative labor markets (w_A), the income or wealth level of faculty from other sources (V_F), and the number of individuals who are qualified to serve as faculty in the given market (N_F):

$$S_F = f(w_F, w_A, V_F, N_F) \qquad (5.4)$$

The market supply and demand curves for faculty then come together to form the market-clearing, or equilibrium, wage rate and employment level for faculty. This is shown in Figure 5.3.

It is important to understand at this point that although faculty members at a given institution are all technically employed by the same institution, they essentially operate in separate labor markets depending on their field and perhaps subfield. This arises because faculty with different terminal degrees will normally be eligible for employment in different fields outside education. As a result, both the wages in alternative labor markets and the number of individuals with qualifications to enter a specific field as a faculty member will vary across fields and disciplines. Thus, one can think of each academic discipline as having separate market supply and demand curves.

Comparative statics can be valuable for examining how changes in the equilibrium wage rate and employment level of faculty would be affected by changes in the labor market. For the labor market demand and supply equilibrium shown in Figure 5.3, for example, comparative statics would attempt to identify how the wage rate and employment level of faculty in a given discipline would be predicted to change as either the market demand or supply curve shifts. When the labor demand curve for faculty shifts to the right (increases), the model shown in Figure 5.3 would predict that faculty wages and employment levels in this field would rise, and vice versa for decreases in labor demand. The labor demand curve for faculty would be predicted to shift outward to the right when any of the following occurs, with examples shown in parentheses:

- The demand for teaching services increases (the institution experiences an increase in enrollments).
- The demand for research services increases (the institution receives a large grant to conduct research).
- The institution's income or wealth increases (there is a rise in the institution's revenues from state appropriations).
- The price of faculty substitutes rises (adjunct faculty or graduate students receive a wage increase).
- The price of faculty complements falls (computer technology falls in price).
- The number of institutions increases (a new community college opens).

Figure 5.3. Equilibrium Wages and Employment in the Academic Labor Market

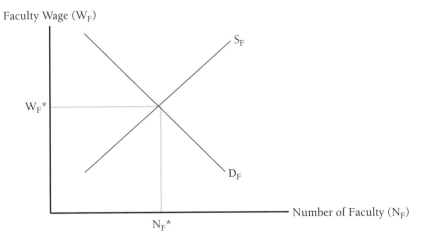

Turning to the labor market supply curve, when the labor supply curve for faculty shifts to the right (increases), the model shown in Figure 5.3 would predict that faculty wages in this field will fall and employment levels will rise, and vice versa for decreases in labor supply. The labor supply curve for faculty would be predicted to shift outward to the right when any of the following occurs, with examples shown in parentheses:

- The wage rate that faculty can earn in external labor markets decreases (average salaries of Ph.D.s in computer science fall).
- There is a decrease in nonlabor income or wealth (a stock market decline reduces faculty pensions and asset holdings).
- The number of individuals who are qualified to be faculty members increases (doctoral programs in sociology produce 10 percent more graduates in the current year than in previous years).

The model shown above is helpful for understanding how general wages are set in academia and how they vary by field. Within each of these markets, however, faculty salaries will likely vary due to the relative contributions that each individual is thought to make to the institution. Economists refer to this contribution as the marginal revenue product of labor (MRP_L), which is the product of the marginal productivity of labor (MP_L) and the marginal revenue from an additional worker (MR_L):

$$MRP_L = MP_L * MR_L \qquad (5.5)$$

For the academic labor market, MP_L represents the change in an institution's productivity due to an additional faculty member (through research, teaching, and service contributions), and MR_L is the change in the institution's total revenues due to the additional faculty member (through enrollments, grants, and so on). Based on this model, an institution would be willing to pay an individual faculty member a salary up to his or her marginal revenue product because for any wage that is below MRP_L, the benefit of hiring the individual exceeds the cost to the institution.

Although the concepts of MP_L, MR_L, and hence MRP_L are difficult to estimate with any degree of precision for faculty, they can be used to understand why faculty who are thought to be more productive are paid more than others. In particular, economists posit that a worker's marginal productivity will be affected by the collective attributes that he or she brings to the labor market. This concept is known as human capital (see Schultz, 1961; Becker, 1964; Mincer, 1974; Paulsen, 2001). Human capital can be affected by factors such as a person's educational attainment (which is why economists refer to education as an investment in one's human capital), work experience, and natural ability.

Taken together, this framework has proven to be invaluable to institutional researchers when doing work relating to faculty compensation and employment. Based on this model, the salaries of individual faculty members at an institution can vary due to any of the factors that change the estimated productivity of faculty or lead to shifts in the supply of labor or the demand for labor, or both. As institutional researchers produce reports on average salaries by department, for example, they can draw on the predictions of this model to understand and explain to administrators how differences in average salaries may be due to variations in external market salaries or the number of new Ph.D.s within fields.

This framework is especially valuable for institutional researchers who are asked to conduct a salary equity study for their institution. These studies usually focus on trying to estimate whether faculty are paid differently based on nonwork-related characteristics such as gender and race/ethnicity (Ashraf, 1996; Barbezat, 1989, 1991, 2002; Ferber, 1974; Hoffman, 1976; Katz, 1973; Ransom and Megdal, 1993; Toutkoushian and Conley, 2005). It is usually the case that the average salary for male faculty exceeds the average for female faculty, and such mean differences could raise concerns within the institution about possible pay discrimination. However, the economic model of labor markets suggests a variety of legitimate reasons that the salaries of faculty within an institution could differ from each other. If this is true, and on average male and female faculty differ in regard to these reasons, then some or possibly all of the average salary differential between the genders could be explained by these legitimate factors.

The way in which this is addressed empirically is to estimate a multiple regression salary model for faculty. The explanatory variables used in such a model typically include controls for factors such as a faculty member's educational attainment, years of prior experience, years of experience at the current institution (seniority), academic field or department, and, when available, research productivity. The multiple regression model is then used to remove the effects of these factors from faculty salaries and determine if there is any remaining difference in average (adjusted) salaries between male and female faculty. All of these factors are chosen based on their connection to the economic models of labor markets and human capital. Without a theoretical framework such as this to help the analyst in deciding which variables to include as controls in the salary model, the exercise of trying to measure pay differences for comparable male and female faculty could be challenged on the grounds that the "legitimate" pay differences are affected too much by the arbitrary choices of control variables made by the institutional researcher.

Part-Time Versus Full-Time Faculty

Finally, another important faculty issue that affects institutional research concerns the use of part-time faculty in academe. Data from the U.S. Department of Education (2004) show a dramatic increase in the reliance on part-time faculty in higher education, with the percentage of instructional faculty in degree-granting institutions rising from 22 percent in 1970 to 46 percent in 2003. This trend has raised concern among education stakeholders regarding the treatment of faculty who work part time and the impacts on students who have less classroom contact with tenure-track faculty. Accordingly, many institutional research offices now report on trends in the percentage of students and courses taught by part-time faculty.

Several economists have examined labor market issues surrounding part-time faculty, including Tuckman (1978), Tuckman and Katz (1981), Tuckman and Pickerill (1988), and Toutkoushian and Bellas (2003). The productivity model described above can also be used to understand aspects of the staffing decisions made by institutions with regard to part-time and full-time faculty. The increased reliance on part-time faculty could reflect a shift in either the demand or supply (or both) for part-time faculty. On the demand side, as individual faculty members must choose how to allocate their time between teaching and research to produce outcomes, so must an institution choose how to use full-time and part-time faculty to achieve its goals. Part-time faculty are essentially a substitute resource for full-time faculty with regard to delivering teaching services for the institution. Because the wages paid to part-time faculty are on average less than the wage paid to full-time faculty per course, part-time faculty may enable the institution to deliver some teaching services at a lower cost. However, because part-time faculty are not as engaged as their full-time counterparts in the research mission of the institution, they are not perfect substitutes, and thus replacing full-time faculty with part-time faculty would most likely reduce the institution's research output.

On the supply side of the labor market, economists would point out that individuals who are hired as part-time faculty must have been willing and able to work at the wages offered by the institution. The fact that most are paid less on a per-course basis than full-time faculty could reflect lower levels of human capital (such as the lower likelihood of holding a terminal degree in their field), lower opportunity costs, or higher preferences for working part time. Educators have noted that part-time faculty are a heterogeneous group, with many different reasons for working on a part-time basis in academe.

Institutional researchers need to understand these issues when helping administrators interpret data that they produce on faculty staffing patterns by full-time status. Those who would argue for more use of part-time faculty as a means of saving money should be cautioned as to the possible negative consequences for producing research and subsequent academic reputation of the institution. Similarly, advocates for less reliance on part-time faculty need to understand that the strategic use of part-time faculty may help an institution balance out its dual mission in teaching and research and that some part-time faculty are working in this capacity because they feel it is in their best interest to do so.

New Directions for Institutional Research • DOI: 10.1002/ir

Conclusion

Institutional research is undergoing a significant shift in the types of work that are expected by professionals in the field. It used to be the case that the primary role of institutional research was to produce data in a consistent and reliable manner for internal and external agencies and then leave it up to them to interpret the information. As information systems improve and the demands on administrators to show accountability rise, institutional researchers are being asked to help administrators understand the implications of the numbers and use them for policymaking. For example, the questions have changed from, "How many of our faculty are employed part time?" to "Do we have too many or too few part-time faculty?"

To answer questions such as this, institutional researchers need to draw on the perspectives of multiple fields, including economics. The tools of economics are valuable in this regard for helping to frame the problems and issues surrounding the use of faculty in academe. To date, the majority of economic work on faculty issues has centered on faculty compensation. The theory of labor markets is also crucial in understanding the ways in which faculty are compensated in academe. Without this framework, it would be nearly impossible for institutional researchers to evaluate the compensation practice of an institution and determine if it is appropriate. This work is important to continue given the findings by Toutkoushian and Conley (2005) and others that significant unexplained wage gaps between male and female faculty still persist in academe.

There are, however, other aspects of faculty work, and hence institutional research on faculty, that can be informed by economics. The economist's model of individual behavior can be used to understand how faculty make decisions about allocating their time between teaching and research and how modifications in the incentive structure might bring about desired changes. The institutional researcher can use this model to explain institutional data on faculty workloads to administrators, describe the likely costs and benefits of changes in time allocation, and provide possible explanations for differences between his or her institution and its peers. As demands for accountability rise within academe, institutions will be hard-pressed to explain to stakeholders why many faculty spend a significant portion of their time outside the classroom. This will call for new measures of productivity that encompass research, teaching, and service; empirical work on the benefits of this work to students and the public; and evaluation of policies to increase rewards for teaching. A second policy issue discussed here that can benefit from economic reasoning is the increasing use of part-time faculty in academe. Toutkoushian and Bellas (2003) showed how the economic framework of supply and demand can be used to help understand a multifaceted issue such as this.

Other faculty-related topics in institutional research could also benefit from economic reasoning. First, many institutional research offices are responsible for working with and reporting data on student evaluations of faculty. Institutions need to understand how various factors influence these evaluations and whether they are good proxy measures of the quality of teaching. Second, little attention has been given to what institutions can do to increase the attractiveness of their institution to prospective faculty members. For example, what is the optimal mix for an institution between fringe benefits and faculty pay? Labor economists refer to these and other non-salary characteristics of jobs as "compensating wage differentials" (Ehrenberg and Smith, 2000). Institutional researchers can use this framework when reporting data on faculty hiring and retention to explore reasons behind the numbers and identify policies to improve hiring and retention.

Economic reasoning is already a central part of the work that institutional researchers conduct on faculty issues. The importance of economics in this area promises to increase as the work of institutional researchers continues to shift away from data reporting and toward analytical issues that are useful for policymaking. We hope that the models described in this chapter give institutional researchers a starting place for seeing how to make this transition successfully.

References

Ashraf, J. "The Influence of Gender on Faculty Salaries in the United States, 1969–89." *Applied Economics,* 1996, *28*(7), 857–864.
Barbezat, D. "Affirmative Action in Higher Education: Have Two Decades Altered Salary Differentials by Sex and Race?" *Research in Labor Economics,* 1989, *10,* 107–156.
Barbezat, D. "Updating Estimates of Male-Female Salary Differentials in the Academic Labor Market." *Economics Letters,* 1991, *36*(2), 191–195.
Barbezat, D. "History of Pay Equity Studies." In R. Toutkoushian (ed.), *Conducting Salary-Equity Studies: Alternative Approaches to Research.* New Directions for Institutional Research, no. 115. San Francisco: Jossey-Bass, 2002.
Becker, G. *Human Capital: A Theoretical and Empirical Analysis with Special Reference to Education.* Cambridge, Mass.: National Bureau of Economic Research, 1964.
Becker, G. "A Theory of the Allocation of Time." *Economic Journal,* 1965, *75,* 493–517.
Becker, W. "The University Professor as Utility Maximizer and Producer of Learning, Research, and Income." *Journal of Human Resources,* 1975, *10*(1), 107–115.
Becker, W. "Professorial Behavior Given a Stochastic Reward Structure." *American Economic Review,* 1979, *69*(5), 1010–1017.
Becker, W. "Behavior and Productivity Implications of Institutional and Project Funding of Research: Comment." *American Journal of Agricultural Economics,* 1982, *64*(3), 595–598.
Bellas, M., and Toutkoushian, R. "Faculty Time Allocations and Research Productivity: Gender, Race and Family Effects." *Review of Higher Education,* 1999, *22*(4), 367–390.
Borjas, G. *Labor Economics.* (2nd ed.) New York: McGraw-Hill, 2000.
Bowen, H., and Schuster, J. *American Professors: A National Resource Imperiled.* New York: Oxford University Press, 1986.
Breneman, D., and Youn, T. (eds.). *Academic Labor Markets and Careers.* New York: Falmer Press, 1988.
Caplow, T., and McGee, R. *The Academic Marketplace.* New York: Basic Books, 1958.
Cartter, A. "The Supply and Demand for College Teachers." *Journal of Human Resources,* 1966, *2*(3), 22–37.

Cartter, A. "Scientific Manpower for 1970–1980." *Science*, 1971, *172*, 132–140.

Cartter, A. "The Academic Labor Market." In M. S. Gordon (ed.), *Higher Education and the Labor Market.* New York: McGraw-Hill, 1974.

Ehrenberg, R., and Smith, R. *Modern Labor Economics: Theory and Public Policy.* (7th ed.) Reading, Mass.: Addison-Wesley, 2000.

Ferber, M. "Professors, Performance, and Rewards." *Industrial Relations*, 1974, *13*(1), 69–77.

Hoffman, E. "Faculty Salaries: Is There Discrimination by Sex, Race, and Discipline?" *American Economic Review*, 1976, *66*(1), 196–198.

Katz, D. "Faculty Salaries, Rates of Promotion, and Productivity at a Larger University." *American Economic Review*, 1973, *63*(3), 469–477.

Lieberman, M., and Hall, R. *Introduction to Economics.* Cincinnati, Ohio: South-Western Publishing, 2000.

McEachern, W. *Economics: A Contemporary Introduction.* (4th ed.) Cincinnati, Ohio: South-Western Publishing, 1997.

Mincer, J. *Schooling, Experience, and Earnings.* Cambridge, Mass.: National Bureau of Economic Research, 1974.

Paulsen, M. "The Economics of Human Capital and Investment in Higher Education." In M. B. Paulsen and J. C. Smart (eds.), *The Finance of Higher Education: Theory, Research, Policy and Practice.* New York: Agathon Press, 2001.

Pindyck, R., and Rubinfeld, D. *Microeconomics.* New York: Macmillan, 1989.

Ransom, M., and Megdal, S. "Sex Differences in the Academic Labor Market in the Affirmative Action Era." *Economics of Education Review*, 1993, *12*(1), 21–43.

Schultz, T. "Investment in Human Capital." *American Economic Review*, 1961, *51*(1), 1–17.

Singell, L., Jr., Lillydahl, J., and Singell, L. "Will Changing Times Change the Allocation of Faculty Time?" *Journal of Human Resources*, 1996, *31*(2), 429–449.

Toutkoushian, R. "What Can Labor Economics Tell Us About the Earnings and Employment Prospects for Faculty?" In J. C. Smart (ed.), *Higher Education: Handbook of Theory and Research.* Norwell, Mass.: Kluwer, 2003.

Toutkoushian, R., and Bellas, M. "The Effect of Part-Time Employment and Gender on Faculty Earnings and Satisfaction: Evidence from the NSOPF:93." *Journal of Higher Education*, 2003, *74*(2), 1–24.

Toutkoushian, R., and Conley, V. "Progress for Women in Academe, But Inequities Persist: Evidence from NSOPF:99." *Research in Higher Education*, 2005, *46*(1), 1–28.

Tuckman, H. *Publication, Teaching, and the Academic Reward Structure.* Lanham, Md.: Lexington Books, 1976.

Tuckman, H. "Who Is Part-Time in Academe?" *AAUP Bulletin*, 1978, *66*, pp. 305–315.

Tuckman, H., and Katz, D. "Estimation of Relative Elasticities of Substitution and Relative Compensation for Part-Time Faculty." *Economics of Education Review*, 1981, *1*(3), 359–366.

Tuckman, H., and Pickerill, K. "Part-Time Faculty and Part-Time Academic Careers." In D. Breneman and T. Youn (eds.), *Academic Labor Markets and Careers.* New York: Falmer Press, 1988.

U.S. Department of Education. *Digest of Education Statistics 2004.* Washington, D.C.: U.S. Department of Education, 2004.

Yuker, H. *Faculty Workload: Research, Theory, and Interpretation.* ASHE-ERIC Higher Education Research Report, no. 10. Washington, D.C.: Association for the Study of Higher Education, 1984.

ROBERT K. TOUTKOUSHIAN *is an associate professor in the Department of Educational Leadership and Policy Studies at Indiana University.*

6

This chapter provides some examples and recommendations for expanding the connections between economics and institutional research.

Economics and Institutional Research: Expanding the Connections and Applications

Michael B. Paulsen, Robert K. Toutkoushian

The natural interactions between advanced training in economics and the conduct of institutional research have yielded many productive relationships and connections between institutional research and the field of economics. In particular, the concepts, models, and methods of microeconomics have proven to be useful when applied to the effective performance of a wide variety of tasks in the area of institutional research (see Chapter One, this volume). Economic concepts are particularly useful to institutional researchers when they assemble and analyze data and present written or oral reports for internal use or for audiences outside the institution in the following topical areas: generating, predicting, and managing institutional revenues (see Chapter Two, this volume); identifying, explaining, comparing, and managing institutional costs (see Chapter Three, this volume); providing informational, analytical, predictive, and evaluative support for the recruitment and retention activities of the enrollment management office (see Chapter Four, this volume); and monitoring and studying the employment, activities, compensation, and performance of faculty and staff (see Chapter Five, this volume).

The previous chapters in this volume have examined the more common and well-established connections between economics and institutional research in each of these specific areas in some detail. Therefore, the primary purpose of this chapter is to provide some examples and recommendations

NEW DIRECTIONS FOR INSTITUTIONAL RESEARCH, no. 132, Winter 2006 © Wiley Periodicals, Inc.
Published online in Wiley InterScience (www.interscience.wiley.com) • DOI: 10.1002/ir.198

for expanding the connections between economics and institutional research (IR) through new or extended uses of economics in future IR applications. The examples discussed are currently less common economics-IR connections than those discussed in previous chapters. Instead, they represent new or emerging applications of economics in IR, based on the application of concepts and models from public sector economics.

Public Support for Higher Education

Both public four-year and two-year institutions of higher education have long depended on state appropriations as a reliable and substantial source of revenue. However, since 1980, the share of institutional revenues accounted for by state appropriations has persistently and substantially decreased, accompanied by concomitant increases in the share of revenue derived from tuition (see Chapter Two; Toutkoushian, 2001). Because of the decreases in the proportion of institutional revenues derived from state appropriations relative to tuition charges, society now bears a diminishing share, while individual students and their families bear an expanding share of the burden of financing a college education (Paulsen, 2000; Thomas and Perna, 2004). Consistent with these trends, contemporary rhetoric about the value of higher education has narrowed its focus from a broader perspective on both private *and* public benefits to a far narrower emphasis on private economic benefits alone, such as better jobs and better pay for college graduates (Baum and Payea, 2004; Institute for Higher Education Policy, 1998).

In an effort to widen the scope of discussion and debate and to once again promote an acute nationwide awareness of both the private *and* the public benefits of higher education, the American Council on Education, which is often viewed as a leader among the many higher education associations and institutions actively engaged in key policy initiatives, launched its Solutions for Our Future program in March 2006. The primary goal of this nationwide campaign is to "increase awareness of the public benefits of higher education" with a "multi-year effort aimed at establishing a dialogue with local communities and policy makers about the broad societal benefits of higher education. . . . This dialogue will focus on specific contributions the local college or university makes to society, and what they can do to better serve their community" (American Council on Education, 2006, pp. 1–2). This is a clarion call for individual institutions of higher education to participate in the Solutions initiative by working to demonstrate to members of their local, state, and regional communities the many ways in which their college or university provides substantial public benefits to society in addition to the private benefits it provides for its students. Several hundred institutions have already established a formal partnership with ACE in this initiative, and the rate of participation is growing.

Some institutional researchers are already involved—and more are likely to become involved in the near future—in the identification, collection, and analysis of data and in the preparation of written and oral reports presenting evidence to demonstrate the wide range of contributions their institutions make in the form of public benefits to society in their local, state, and regional communities. Through their understanding and application of some key concepts from the area of public sector economics, institutional researchers can better inform their own efforts in performing each of these sets of tasks, as well as help administrators with whom they work to better understand the context, rationale, and critical importance of demonstrating the public benefits of higher education at their respective colleges and universities.

Public Sector Economics and the Public Benefits of Higher Education

In relation to higher education, public sector economics deals primarily with the role of government and the appropriateness of public investment in higher education, particularly in the form of subsidies to students or institutions that affect students' investment decisions regarding participation in higher education (Baum, 2004; Paulsen, 2001). Public sector economists consider a number of marketplace characteristics to determine whether there are one or more market conditions that indicate market failure. When market failure occurs, a competitive market would produce an amount of goods and services that would be inconsistent with a socially efficient allocation of resources from society's point of view. In these cases, it is appropriate and necessary for the public sector, or government, to intervene in the marketplace with policies that will bear on consumer and producer behavior toward the goal of a more socially efficient allocation of society's resources (Bruce, 2001; Hyman, 2002; Musgrave and Musgrave, 1984; Stiglitz, 2000; Weimer and Vining, 2005).

In higher education, one condition of particular importance for justifying government intervention in the market with public policies is evidence that substantial public or external benefits are created, in addition to the private or internal benefits that accrue to individual students who invest in college (Breneman and Nelson, 1981; Geske and Cohn, 1998; Halstead, 1974; Paulsen, 2001). When students decide how much to invest in higher education, they consider only the private or internal benefits of their investment—such as better jobs and better pay—that accrue to and are captured by only the students themselves. However, in the market for higher education, there is documented evidence that students' investments in higher education also result in substantial public benefits, or *positive externalities* (Baum and Payea, 2004, 2005; Bowen, 1977; Carnegie Commission on Higher Education, 1973; Fatima and Paulsen, 2004; Haveman and Wolfe, 1984; Institute for Higher Education Policy, 1998, 2005; Leslie and Brinkman, 1988; Michael, 1982; Paulsen and Fatima, 2005).

Positive externalities are public benefits that accrue to members of society in general and are therefore external to individual students' investment decisions (Paulsen and Peseau, 1989). An example of an unambiguous public or external benefit is an increase in the overall productivity of a state's workforce that leads to increases in incomes for all workers even if they do not have a college education (Baumol, Blackman, and Wolff, 1989; Fatima and Paulsen, 2004; Paulsen and Fatima, 2005). The perceptions of individual students regarding the value of the private or internal benefits they will acquire from higher education determine their willingness to pay for higher education. Similarly, the perceptions of society regarding the value of the public or external benefits that accrue to them determine their willingness to pay for students' investment in higher education. In the presence of positive externalities, the college enrollment decisions of individual students, which are based solely on the private or internal benefits that accrue only to them, will not result in a socially optimal level of investment in higher education. Instead, the combination of all students' decisions will result in an underinvestment in higher education. Under these circumstances, public investment in higher education in the form of subsidies like state appropriations to institutions or grants to students is necessary and justified to promote a more socially efficient level of investment in higher education (Baum, 2004; Paulsen, 2001).

Externalities, Private and Social Demand, and Optimal Investment in Higher Education: A Diagrammatic Exposition. Figure 6.1 illustrates the theoretical framework that public sector economists use to identify the socially optimal level of investment in higher education, based on the relationships between the private demand for higher education of individual students (D_P), the demand for external benefits by society (D_E), and the

Figure 6.1. Externalities, Private and Social Demand, and Optimal Investment in Higher Education

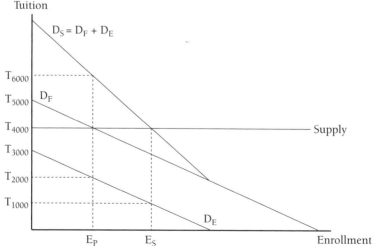

overall social demand for higher education enrollment ($D_S = D_P + D_E$) (see Paulsen, 2001). In Figure 6.1, the horizontal supply curve is what economists refer to as perfectly elastic, and it indicates that for the overall market of public four-year institutions, there is enough capacity to enroll all students who wish to attend at the average price at these institutions (T_{4000}). The height of D_P for various quantities of enrollment indicates students' willingness to pay for the private or internal benefits of college. The intersection of D_P and Supply occurs at price T_{4000}. This is a level of tuition at which E_P students are willing to pay to enroll and for which suppliers are willing to provide E_P places for students. The quantity of enrollment, E_P, and market price, T_{4000}, define what the market equilibrium would be if external benefits were completely ignored.

However, the height of D_E for various quantities of enrollment indicates society's willingness to pay for the external benefits of college. As Figure 6.1 shows, when E_P students are enrolled and willing to pay T_{4000}, society is willing to pay another T_{2000} for all the external benefits that would be diffused across the population. Clearly, in the presence of these externalities, E_P is not the socially optimum enrollment; it is the enrollment that would occur in the market if society's willingness to pay for external benefits were completely ignored. Economists identify the socially optimal level of enrollment by vertically summing, across all quantities of enrollment, the willingness to pay for the private or internal benefits of college enrollment by individual students, D_P, and society's willingness to pay for external benefits of college enrollment, D_E, yielding the overall social demand (D_S) for higher education enrollment ($D_S = D_P + D_E$). Overall social demand, D_S, intersects Supply at what is the socially optimal quantity of enrollment, E_S. If no public policies are used to intervene in this market, the resulting underinvestment in higher education would equal the difference $E_S - E_P$. Sufficient subsidization of institutions or students can move the equilibrium quantity of enrollment from E_P to E_S in Figure 6.1, where E_S is the socially optimal level of enrollment.

Evidence of Public Benefits at the National, State, and Institutional Levels. Recently, in an effort to expand and broaden awareness of both public and private benefits of college education, a number of studies have been conducted to provide empirical evidence of the nature and magnitude of the public benefits, both tangible and intangible, of investment in higher education (Baum and Payea, 2004, 2005; Fatima and Paulsen, 2004; Institute for Higher Education Policy, 1998, 2005; Midwestern Higher Education Compact, 2005; Paulsen and Fatima, 2005; Williams and Swail, 2005). However, these studies have focused entirely on evidence of public benefits at the national, regional, or state levels, largely ignoring the level of the individual institution and its unique contribution of public benefits to its communities.

The need for evidence of public benefits at the institutional level is where the expertise, experiences, and perspectives of institutional researchers are invaluable. When institutional researchers work to assemble and report on evidence of the public benefits of higher education at their own institutions, they could inform their initial investigations by collecting and examining institutional data on the kinds of public benefits that have been observed and reported in the aggregate-level studies cited above. For example, analysts have found evidence that higher education produces public benefits in the following areas: higher tax revenues, greater workforce productivity, greater workforce flexibility and adaptability to change, lower levels of unemployment and poverty and less reliance on government assistance programs, lower crime rates and rates of incarceration, less smoking and better overall health, more charitable giving, more community service, more volunteerism, increased participation in voting, more blood donation, greater social cohesion, and greater appreciation of diversity in society. To support continued or increased public funding of higher education, institutional researchers can contribute important studies that estimate the nature and magnitude of the public benefits generated by investment in higher education at their own institutions. These studies could produce evidence of any of the types of public benefits identified above, as well as additional ones that are specific or unique to their own institutions.

The measurement of the public benefits of higher education is not a straightforward matter. Instead, such measurement can be challenging for a number of reasons. First, some of the constructs that are accepted and potentially important indicators of public benefits are not readily quantifiable. A number of indicators of intangible public benefits do not have naturally occurring units or scales of measurement associated with them. For example, how would one measure qualitative indicators of the public benefits of higher education such as "social cohesion" or "appreciation of diversity"? Second, the kinds of data needed to measure many forms of public benefits are often not readily available in an existing data warehouse on campus and may require considerable time and a substantial budget to collect. Third, even for indicators of public benefits that can be observed, such as crime rates, charitable giving, or volunteer behavior, it may be difficult to conclusively demonstrate that variation or differences in these indicators are due to higher education.

Nevertheless, there are a number of workable ways to address these challenges, albeit each has notable limitations. We describe an example here. In order to address the challenges described above, institutional researchers can use some well-crafted survey research. First, they can survey their own students, both while they are still students and after they become graduates, including items on the survey to collect students' and graduates' self-report of their perceptions, behaviors, and experiences about a wide range of possible indicators of public benefits of higher education. The range of indicators for which items are written can include many of those listed above from previous research, such as charitable giving, voting, volunteer behavior, and many more, as well as others that are unique to institutional researchers' own institutions and their own local, state, and regional communities.

There are also some reasonable, though far from ideal, ways to address the challenge of establishing evidence that the public benefits observed are actually due to investment in higher education. One way is to include survey items that ask students and graduates to report their perceptions of the manner and extent to which the indicators of public benefits assessed on the survey are related to the experiences and outcomes of their college educations. Another way is to select a sample from the general population that is representative of the relevant local or state communities believed to be recipients of public benefits of a particular institution or set of institutions and administer a similar survey to them. This sample could include those with college educations and those with no postsecondary educational experiences. With these data, institutional researchers could make a series of comparisons to assess differences in indicators of public benefits between those in the general population with no college experience and those with college educations, and between these two groups and those students and graduates from the institutional researchers' own institutions. Finally, in order to address the challenges of limited time and budgets, institutional researchers from multiple institutions, particularly those serving similar local or state communities, might choose to join forces and resources to develop and administer the surveys and analyze the data.

Economic Impact Studies. One area in which the measurement of public benefits has proven to be less problematic is in the use of economic impact studies to estimate the public economic benefits due to the presence of a college or university in a local or state community. After the large number of economic impact studies that were conducted in the 1970s and 1980s (see Leslie and Brinkman, 1988), such efforts have become much less common, and earlier ones have become dated and in many instances forgotten. Economic impact studies estimate the impact of either a single institution of higher education or a group of institutions on economic activity in the local, state, or regional economies. Therefore, economic impact studies offer productive frameworks and particularly fruitful opportunities for institutional researchers to design and conduct studies that demonstrate some of the unique ways in which their own institutions contribute public economic benefits in their own local or state economies.

Most economic impact studies have used some version of the traditional methods developed by Caffrey and Isaacs (1971). In their review of research on the economic impact of higher education in local and regional economies, Leslie and Slaughter (1992) found that each $1 million of expenditure from four-year college budgets generates an additional $1.8 million of spending by businesses and an additional fifty-three jobs. Leslie and Brinkman (1988) reported similar findings from their review: each $1 million of expenditure from public college budgets generates an additional $1.5 to $1.6 million in business volume and an additional fifty-nine jobs in the local economy.

Evidence of public benefits based on economic impact studies has typically received a more welcome response from state and local policymakers than efforts to measure the value to society of less quantifiable public benefits. As part of the national campaign to heighten the nation's awareness of the public benefits of higher education, it is likely that institutional researchers will be asked to conduct new economic impact studies, thereby providing another potent way for them, and the administrators with whom they work, to demonstrate the extent of the public economic benefits that directly or indirectly result from the presence of their institutions in local communities.

Institutional researchers can apply concepts and models from public sector economics to guide their conduct of studies to demonstrate the nature and magnitude of a wide variety of public benefits—both tangible and intangible, and both economic and social—to local and state communities that are generated by their own institutions. In addition, when institutional researchers prepare oral or written reports on the evidence of public benefits in their studies, as part of their communication with internal audiences—such as the administrators with whom they work—or as part of their communication with external audiences of state and local agencies and policymakers, they can use concepts from public sector economics to clarify the rationale and central importance of articulating the evidence of the public benefits of investment in higher education at their respective colleges and universities.

References

American Council on Education. *American Council on Education Launches First-of-Its-Kind Campaign on Benefits of Higher Education to Society.* Washington, D.C.: American Council on Education, 2006.

Baum, S. *A Primer on Economics for Financial Aid Professionals.* New York: College Board, 2004.

Baum, S., and Payea, K. *Education Pays: The Benefits of Higher Education for Individuals and Society.* New York: College Board, 2004.

Baum, S., and Payea, K. *Education Pays: Update 2005.* New York: College Board, 2005.

Baumol, W. J., Blackman, S., and Wolff, E. *Productivity and American Leadership.* Cambridge, Mass.: MIT Press, 1989.

Bowen, H. *Investment in Learning: The Individual and Social Value of American Higher Education.* San Francisco: Jossey-Bass, 1977.

Breneman, D., and Nelson, S. *Financing Community Colleges: An Economic Perspective.* Washington, D.C.: Brookings Institution, 1981.

Bruce, N. *Public Finance and the American Economy.* Reading, Mass.: Addison-Wesley, 2001.

Caffrey, J., and Isaacs, H. *Estimating the Impact of a College or University on the Local Economy.* Washington, D.C.: American Council on Education, 1971.

Carnegie Commission on Higher Education. *Higher Education: Who Pays? Who Benefits? Who Should Pay?* New York: McGraw-Hill, 1973.

Fatima, N., and Paulsen, M. "Higher Education and State Workforce Productivity in the 1990s." *Thought and Action: The NEA Higher Education Journal,* 2004, *20*(1), 75–94.

Geske, T. G., and Cohn, E. "Why Is a High School Diploma No Longer Enough? The Economic and Social Benefits of Higher Education." In R. Fossey and M. Bateman (eds.), *Condemning Students to Debt: College Loans and Public Policy.* New York: Teachers College Press, 1998.

Halstead, D. *Statewide Planning in Higher Education.* Washington, D.C.: U.S. Government Printing Office, 1974.

Haveman, R., and Wolfe, B. "Schooling and Economic Well-being: The Role of Nonmarket Effects." *Journal of Human Resources,* 1984, *19*(3), 377–407.

Hyman, D. *Public Finance: A Contemporary Application of Theory to Policy.* Orlando, Fla.: Harcourt, 2002.

Institute for Higher Education Policy. *Reaping the Benefits: Defining the Public and Private Value of Going to College.* Washington, D.C.: Institute for Higher Education Policy, 1998.

Institute for Higher Education Policy. *The Investment Payoff: A Fifty-State Analysis of the Public and Private Benefits of Higher Education.* Washington, D.C.: Institute for Higher Education Policy, 2005.

Leslie, L., and Brinkman, P. *The Economic Value of Higher Education.* New York: ACE/Macmillan, 1988.

Leslie, L., and Slaughter, S. "Higher Education and Regional Economic Development." In W. Becker and D. Lewis (eds.), *The Economics of American Higher Education.* Norwell, Mass.: Kluwer, 1992.

Michael, R. T. "Measuring Non-Monetary Benefits of Education: A Survey." In W. McMahon and T. Geske (eds.), *Financing Education: Overcoming Inefficiency and Inequity.* Urbana: University of Illinois Press, 1982.

Midwestern Higher Education Compact. *Investment Payoff: The Benefits of a Higher Education in the Midwestern States.* Minneapolis, Minn.: MHEC, 2005.

Musgrave, R., and Musgrave, P. *Public Finance in Theory and Practice.* New York: McGraw-Hill, 1984.

Paulsen, M. "Economic Perspectives on Rising College Tuition: A Theoretical and Empirical Exploration." In J. Smart (ed.), *Higher Education: Handbook of Theory and Research.* New York: Agathon Press, 2000.

Paulsen, M. "The Economics of the Public Sector: The Nature and Role of Public Policy in the Finance of Higher Education" In M. Paulsen and J. Smart (eds.), *The Finance of Higher Education: Theory, Research, Policy and Practice.* New York: Agathon Press, 2001.

Paulsen, M., and Fatima, N. "Higher Education and Growth in State Workforce Productivity: Evidence on the Public Benefits of College Education." Paper presented at the Annual Conference of the Association for the Study of Higher Education, Philadelphia, 2005.

Paulsen, M., and Peseau, B. "Ten Essential Economic Concepts Every Administrator Should Know." *Journal for Higher Education Management,* 1989, 5(1), 9–17.

Stiglitz, J. *Economics of the Public Sector.* New York: Norton, 2000.

Thomas, S., and Perna, L. "The Opportunity Agenda: A Reexamination of Postsecondary Reward and Opportunity." In J. Smart (ed.), *Higher Education: Handbook of Theory and Research.* Norwell, Mass.: Kluwer, 2004.

Toutkoushian, R. "Trends in Revenues and Expenditures for Public and Private Higher Education." In M. Paulsen and J. Smart (eds.), *The Finance of Higher Education: Theory, Research, Policy and Practice.* New York: Agathon Press, 2001.

Weimer, D., and Vining, A. *Policy Analysis: Concepts and Practice,* Upper Saddle River, N.J.: Pearson/Prentice Hall, 2005.

Williams, A., and Swail, W. *Is More Better? The Impact of Postsecondary Education on the Economic and Social Well-Being of American Society.* Washington, D.C.: Educational Policy Institute, 2005.

MICHAEL B. PAULSEN is professor of higher education in the Department of Educational Policy and Leadership Studies at The University of Iowa.

ROBERT K. TOUTKOUSHIAN is associate professor of education in the Department of Educational Leadership and Policy Studies at Indiana University.

INDEX

Aaron, H., 21
Academic labor market, equilibrium wages and employment in, 87 Fig.5.3
ACE. *See* American Council on Education
Ahlburg, D., 60, 70
Allen, R. H., 45, 51
American Council on Education (ACE), 96
Arnold, R., 22
Ashraf, J., 89
Asker, E., 60

Baker, B. D., 54, 56
Barbezat, D., 89
Baum, S., 18, 96–99
Baumol, W. J., 54, 55, 98
Bayh-Dole Act (1980), 25
Becker, G., 21, 22, 33, 60, 81, 88
Becker, W., 60, 62, 83
Belfield, C., 21
Bell, A., 59
Bellas, M., 81, 90, 91
Berg, D., 69
Berger, J. B., 56
Blackman, S.A.B., 54, 55, 98
Blaug, M., 21
Blumenstyk, G., 39
Bok, D., 25
Borden, V.M.H., 50
Borjas, G., 85
Bowen, H., 18, 20, 25, 34, 35, 54, 85–86, 97
Braxton, J., 60
Breneman, D., 34, 35, 85–86, 97
Brinkman, P. T., 43, 45, 48, 51, 54, 64, 97, 101
Bruce, N., 97
Budak, S., 31

Caffrey, J., 101
Cantor, N., 27
Caplow, T., 85–86
Carbone, J., 30
Carnegie Commission on Higher Education, 97
Cartter, A., 85–86

Caruthers, J. K., 55
Chapman, R., 60
Cheslock, J. J., 25
Clotfelter, C. T., 54, 67–68
Cobb-Douglass production function, 82
Cohn, E., 21, 97
Collins, E., 21
Competitive markets: economic theory of, 15–19; equilibrium in, 16 fig. 1.7
Conley, V., 89, 91
Consumer Price Index (CPI), 32, 33
Coomes, M., 59
Coopersmith, G., 60
Corey, S., 37
Costs: average, 49–51; and average and marginal cost curves, 46 fig. 3.1; and cost-related tasks for institutional researchers, 44–45; determining, 47–52; economic model of, 45–47; fixed *versus* variable, 52; increasing, 54–57; interpreting and comparing, 52–54; marginal, 51
Courant, P., 27

Davis, J., 70
Delaware Study of Costs and Productivity, 49
DesJardins, S., 11, 59, 60, 67, 69–71
Dey, E. L., 56
Dubner, S., 22
Dundar, H., 49, 60

Econometrics, 6
Economic approach, 6–10
Economic concepts: overview of, 5–22; use of, in research on costs, 43–57
Economic theory: of individual behavior, 10–19; of markets, 15–19; of organizational behavior, 19–20
Ehrenberg, R., 21, 38, 39, 54, 83, 92
Elasticity, 63–67; and revenue relationships, 64 fig. 4.2; and total revenue changes given price changes in elastic and inelastic ranges, 65 fig. 4.3
Enrollment management, using economic concepts to inform, 59–72

Equilibrium price, 16
Externalities, 18, 97–98

Faculty: categories of institutional research on, 76–85; economic contributions to institutional research on, 75–92; and economic theory of time allocation and productivity, 81–85; external reporting on, 76; internal analysis of, 77–80; internal reporting on, 76–77; labor market, 85–89; part-time *versus* full-time, 89–90; scholarly research on, 80–87; time allocation, 13 fig.1.5, 70; work activities, data availability of, 79 table 5.2
Fatima, N., 18, 97–99
Ferber, M., 89
Financial Accounting Standards Board, 31
Frank, R., 6, 8, 14, 19, 35
Freakonomics (Levitt and Dubner), 22
Free Application for Student Assistance, 69
Friedman, M., 8

Garvin, D., 18, 21
General Accounting Standards Board, 32
Geske, T., 21, 97
Getz, M., 48–50
Grapevine Survey on State Tax Appropriations to Higher Education (Palmer), 32
Gumport, P. J., 54
Gunter, D., 32, 33

Hall, R., 81
Halstead, D., 97
Harter, J.F.B., 48–50, 53, 54, 56
Hausman, D., 21
Haveman, R., 97
Heller, D., 8, 17, 64, 66, 70
Hendel, D., 60
Higher education: costs, 43–57; and evidence of public benefits at national, state, and institutional levels, 43–57; examples of economic problems in, 7 table 1.1; public sector economics and public benefits of, 97–102; public support for, 96–98
Higher Education General Information Survey (HEGIS), 30, 31
Higher Education Price Index (HEPI), 32, 33
Hirshleifer, J., 21, 61, 63

Hoenack, S. A., 21, 47, 62, 69
Hoffmann, E., 89
Hollis, P., 33
Hopkins, S., 20
Hossler, D., 59, 60, 70
Hovey, H., 33, 34, r1
Hoxby, C., 21
Hu, S., 60
Hubbell, L., 36, 70
Human capital, 88, 89
Hyatt, J., 50
Hyman, D., 97

Indiana University, 66–67
Indifference curve, 10
Institute for Higher Education Policy, 96, 97, 99
Institutional research: applying economics to, on higher education revenues, 25–40; expanding connections and applications of economics and, 95–102; overview of economic concepts, models, and methods for, 5–22; and using economic concepts on higher education costs, 43–57
Integrated Postsecondary Education Data (IPEDS), 30, 31
Isaacs, H., 101

Jackson, G., 60
Jakubson, G., 39
James, E., 26, 48, 55, 56
Johnes, G., 21, 54
Johnes, J., 54
Jones, D., 33, 34

K-12 education, 33
Kane, T., 8, 32, 33, 60
Katz, D., 89, 90
Keene State College (New Hampshire), 84, 85
Kohn, M., 60

Lapovsky, L., 36, 70
Layzell, D. T., 55
Leslie, L. L., 54, 56, 64, 97, 101
Levitt, S., 22
Lewis, D. R., 49, 60
Lieberman, M., 81
Lillydahl, J., 81

Macroeconomics, 6
Mankiw, G., 6, 15, 21, 28, 35
Manski, C., 60

Marginal analysis, 14; optimal decision making using, 15 fig.1.6
Marginalism, 14
Market demand curve, 16
Martin, R., 36
Massy, W., 27, 28
Maurice, S., 61, 67
McCall, B., 60, 70
McEachern, W., 6, 21, 81, 83, 85
McGee, R., 85–86
McPherson, M., 30, 34, 70
Medicaid, 33
Megdal, S., 89
Michael, R. T., 97
Microeconomics, 6
Middaugh, M. F., 49, 50, 54, 56
Midwestern Higher Education Compact, 99
Milam, J. F., 56
Mincer, J., 21, 88
Morphew, C. C., 54, 56
Mundel, D., 60
Musgrave, P., 97
Musgrave, R., 97

National Center for Education Statistics, 31, 32
National Commission on the Cost of Higher Education, 54
Nelson, S., 97
Neuberger, E., 26

Optimization process, 6; depiction of, in economic models, 8 fig.1.1
Orszag, P., 32, 33

Palmer, J., 32
Paulsen, M. B., 5, 8, 14, 16, 18, 20, 21, 60, 88, 95–99
Payea, K., 18, 96, 97, 99
Perlman, R., 21
Perna, L., 96
Peseau, B., 97
Pickerill, K., 90
Pindyck, R., 6, 10, 14, 15, 21, 81
Plymouth State College (New Hampshire), 84, 85
Price discrimination, 69–71
Price elasticity, demand, supply, and variation in, 17 fig. 1.8
Production possibilities frontier (PPF), 9
Productivity, 81–85
Public sector economics, 97–102
Pusser, B., 54

Ransom, M., 89
Rational behavior, 11
Redd, K., 36
Revenues, higher education: and considerations for specific revenue sources, 30–39; and general revenue considerations, 26–30; and general revenue shares by source, 31 table 2.1; and institutional differences, 30; marginal, 28–29; and state appropriations, 32–34; and tuition revenue, 34–38
Rhoades, G., 25, 54, 56
Rizzo, M., 33, 39
Rooney, P. M., 50
Rothschild, M., 20
Rubinfeld, D., 6, 10, 14, 15, 21, 81

Schapiro, M., 30, 34, 70
Schmit, J., 60
Schultz, T., 21, 88
Schuster, J., 85–86
Selingo, J., 34
Siegfried, J. J., 48–50
Simpson, W. A., 45
Singell, L., 81
Singell, L., Jr., 81
Slaughter, S., 25, 101
Smart, J., 21
Smith, A., 5
Smith, R., 21, 85, 92
Smithson, C., 61, 67
Spence, M., 21
Sperber, W. E., 45
St. John, E., 60, 70, 71
State appropriations, 32–34
Stiglitz, J., 21, 97
Strout, E., 30, 38
Supply and demand, 15–16, 61, 65 fig. 4.3; and changes in quantity demanded versus changes or shifts in demand, 62 fig. 4.1; and and supply-side considerations, 67–69
Swail, W., 99

Thomas, S., 96
Thomas, T. J., 50
Thurow, L., 21
Time allocation, 81–85
Toutkoushian, R. K., 5, 11, 18, 19, 21, 30, 32, 33, 48, 51, 53, 60, 69, 75, 81, 85, 86, 89, 91, 95, 96
Tuckman, H., 85–86, 90
Tuition revenue, 34–38; impact of tuition increases on, 37 fig. 2.2

United States Department of Education, 89–90
University of Illinois, 66–67
University of Iowa, 66–67
University of Minnesota, 70
University of New Hampshire, 84, 85
University System of New Hampshire, 84, 85; data on faculty teaching activities in, 85 table 5.3

Venti, S., 60
Vesper, N., 60
Vining, A., 97

Wade, J. A., 48–50, 54, 56
Watkins, T. G., 48–50, 53, 54, 56

Weathersby, G., 60
Wegner, G., 27, 28
Weiler, W., 60, 62, 69, 71
Weimer, D., 97
White, L., 20
Williams, A., 99
Winston, G., 18, 30, 70
Wisconsin, 70
Wise, D., 60
Wolfe, B., 97
Wolff, E., 98

Youn, T., 85–86
Yuker, H., 81

Zemsky, R., 27, 28

Back Issue/Subscription Order Form

Copy or detach and send to:

Jossey-Bass, A Wiley Imprint, 989 Market Street, San Francisco CA 94103-1741

Call or fax toll-free: Phone 888-378-2537 6:30AM – 3PM PST; Fax 888-481-2665

Back Issues: Please send me the following issues at $29 each
(Important: please include ISBN number for each issue.)

_____

_____

_____

$ _____   Total for single issues

$ _____   SHIPPING CHARGES: SURFACE   Domestic Canadian
                                                First Item $5.00 $6.00
                                                Each Add'l Item $3.00 $1.50
                  For next-day and second-day delivery rates, call the number listed above.

Subscriptions   Please __ start __ renew my subscription to *New Directions for Institutional Research* for the year 2_____at the following rate:

U.S.	__ Individual $80	__ Institutional $185
Canada	__ Individual $80	__ Institutional $225
All Others	__ Individual $104	__ Institutional $269

Online subscriptions are available via Wiley InterScience!

**For more information about online subscriptions visit
www.wileyinterscience.com**

$ _____   Total single issues and subscriptions (Add appropriate sales tax for your state for single issue orders. No sales tax for U.S. subscriptions. Canadian residents, add GST for subscriptions and single issues.)

__Payment enclosed (U.S. check or money order only)

__VISA __ MC __ AmEx # _____ Exp. Date _____

Signature _____ Day Phone _____

__ Bill Me (U.S. institutional orders only. Purchase order required.)

Purchase order # _____
                 Federal Tax ID13559302   **GST 89102 8052**

Name _____

Address _____

_____

Phone _____ E-mail _____

For more information about Jossey-Bass, visit our Web site at www.josseybass.com

OTHER TITLES AVAILABLE IN THE
NEW DIRECTIONS FOR INSTITUTIONAL RESEARCH SERIES
Robert K. Toutkoushian, Editor-in-Chief

IR131   Data Mining in Action: Case Studies of Enrollment Management
         Jing Luan, Chun-Mei Zhao
         Data mining has great potential to enhance institutional research. Six case
         studies in this volume employed data mining for solving real-world prob-
         lems in enrollment yield, retention, transfer-outs, utilization of advanced-
         placement scores, predicting graduation rates, and more. Discusses data
         mining vs. traditional statistics, debunks the myths, and highlights the need
         for individual pattern recognition and customized treatment of students.
         ISBN: 0-7879-9426-X

IR 130   Reframing Persistence Research to Improve Academic Success
         Edward P. St. John, Michael Wilkerson
         This volume proposes and tests new collaborations between institutional
         researchers and others on campus who are engaged in breaking down
         barriers to academic success, especially for minorities and nontraditional
         students. What if traditional recommendations aren't effective? Chapters
         review prior research and best practices, then investigate new approaches to
         assessment, action research, action inquiry, and evaluation. Lessons learned
         can inform strategies of administrators, faculty, and everyone interested in
         improving success for all students.
         ISBN: 0-7879-8759-X

IR129   Analyzing Faculty Work and Rewards: Using Boyer's Four Domains of
         Scholarship
         John M. Braxton
         Boyer's four domains—scholarships of discovery, application, integration, and
         teaching—influence and define scholars as their professional roles, career
         stages, and research goals change. This volume offers practical suggestions for
         academic reward structure, graduate school preparation, and state policy.
         ISBN: 0-7879-8674-7

IR128   Workforce Development and Higher Education: A Strategic Role for
         Institutional Research
         Richard A. Voorhees, Lee Harvey
         Workforce development is a growing area for higher education. This volume
         examines its conceptual underpinnings from an international perspective, and
         it provides practical institutional case studies and specific techniques for
         gauging the market potential for new instructional programs. It discusses
         suggested projects and studies for IR personnel to consider on their campuses.
         ISBN: 0-7879-8365-9

IR127   Survey Research: Emerging Issues
         Paul D. Umbach
         Demands for accountability are forcing colleges and universities to conduct
         more high-quality surveys to gauge institutional effectiveness. New
         technologies are improving survey implementation as well as researchers'
         ability to effectively analyze data. This volume examines these emerging
         issues in a rapidly changing environment and highlights lessons learned
         from past research.
         ISBN: 0-7879-8329-2

IR126   **Enhancing Alumni Research: European and American Perspectives**
David J. Weerts, Javier Vidal
The increasing globalization of higher education has made it easy to compare problems, goals, and tools associated with conducting alumni research worldwide. This research is also being used to learn about the impact, purposes, and successes of higher education. This volume will help institutional leaders use alumni research to respond to the increasing demands of state officials, accrediting agencies, employers, prospective students, parents, and the general public.
ISBN: 0-7879-8228-8

IR125   **Minority Retention: What Works?**
Gerald H. Gaither
Examines some of the best policies, practices, and procedures to achieve greater diversity and access, while controlling costs and maintaining quality. Looks at institutions that are majority-serving, tribal, Hispanic-serving, and historically black. Emphasizes that the key to retention is in the professional commitment of faculty and staff to student-centered efforts, and includes practical ideas adaptable to different institutional goals.
ISBN: 0-7879-7974-0

IR124   **Unique Campus Contexts: Insights for Research and Assessment**
Jason E. Lane, M. Christopher Brown II
Summarizes what we know about professional schools, transnational campuses, proprietary schools, religious institutions, and corporate universities. As more students take advantage of these specialized educational environments, conducting meaningful research becomes a challenge. The authors argue for the importance of educational context and debunk the one-size-fits-all approach to assessment, evaluation, and research. Effective institutional measures of inquiry, benchmarks, and indicators must be congruent with the mission, population, and function of each unique campus context.
ISBN: 0-7879-7973-2

IR123   **Successful Strategic Planning**
Michael J. Dooris, John M. Kelley, James F. Trainer
Explains the value of strategic planning in higher education to improve conditions and meet missions (hiring better faculty, recruiting stronger students, upgrading facilities, improving programs, acquiring resources), and what planning tools and methodologies have been used at various campuses. Goes beyond the activity of planning to investigate successful ways to implement and infuse strategic plans throughout the organization. Case studies from various campuses show different ways to achieve success.
ISBN: 0-7879-7792-6

IR122   **Assessing Character Outcomes in College**
Jon C. Dalton, Terrence R. Russell, Sally Kline
Examines several perspectives on the role of higher education in developing students' character, and illustrates approaches to defining and assessing character outcomes. Moral, civic, ethical, and spiritual development are key aspects of students' growth and experience in college, so how can educators encourage good values and assess their impact?
ISBN: 0-7879-7791-8

IR121   **Overcoming Survey Research Problems**
Stephen R. Porter
As demand for survey research has increased, survey response rates have decreased. This volume examines an array of survey research problems and

best practices, from both the literature and field practitioners, to provide solutions to increase response rates while controlling costs. Discusses administering longitudinal studies, doing surveys on sensitive topics such as student drug and alcohol use, and using new technologies for survey administration.
ISBN: 0-7879-7477-3

IR120   **Using Geographic Information Systems in Institutional Research**
Daniel Teodorescu
Exploring the potential of geographic information systems (GIS) applications in higher education administration, this issue introduces IR professionals and campus administrators to a powerful presentation and analysis tool. Chapters explore the benefits of working with the spatial component of data in recruitment, admissions, facilities, alumni development, and other areas, with examples of actual GIS applications from several higher education institutions.
ISBN: 0-7879-7281-9

IR119   **Maximizing Revenue in Higher Education**
F. King Alexander, Ronald G. Ehrenberg
This volume presents edited versions of some of the best articles from a forum on institutional revenue generation sponsored by the Cornell Higher Education Research Institute. The chapters provide different perspectives on revenue generation and how institutions are struggling to find an appropriate balance between meeting public expectations and maximizing private market forces. The insights provided about options and alternatives will enable campus leaders, institutional researchers, and policymakers to better understand evolving patterns in public and private revenue reliance.
ISBN: 0-7879-7221-5

IR118   **Studying Diverse Institutions: Contexts, Challenges, and Considerations**
M. Christopher Brown II, Jason E. Lane
This volume examines the contextual and methodological issues pertaining to studying diverse institutions (including women's colleges, tribal colleges, and military academies), and provides effective and useful approaches for higher education administrators, institutional researchers and planners, policymakers, and faculty seeking to better understand students in postsecondary education. It also offers guidelines to asking the right research questions, employing the appropriate research design and methods, and analyzing the data with respect to the unique institutional contexts.
ISBN: 0-7879-6990-7

IR117   **Unresolved Issues in Conducting Salary-Equity Studies**
Robert K. Toutkoushian
Chapters discuss the issues surrounding how to use faculty rank, seniority, and experience as control variables in salary-equity studies. Contributors review the challenges of conducting a salary-equity study for nonfaculty administrators and staff—who constitute the majority of employees, even in academic institutions—and examine the advantages and disadvantages of using hierarchical linear modeling to measure pay equity. They present a case-study approach to illustrate the political and practical challenges that researchers often face when conducting a salary-equity study for an institution. This is a companion volume to *Conducting Salary-Equity Studies: Alternative Approaches to Research* (IR115).
ISBN: 0-7879-6863-3

United States Postal Service
Statement of Ownership, Management, and Circulation

1. Publication Title	2. Publication Number	3. Filing Date
New Directions For Institutional Research	0 2 7 1 _ 0 5 7 9	10/1/06

4. Issue Frequency	5. Number of Issues Published Annually	6. Annual Subscription Price
Quarterly	4	$185.00

7. Complete Mailing Address of Known Office of Publication *(Not printer) (Street, city, county, state, and ZIP+4)*

Wiley Subscription Services, Inc. at Jossey-Bass, 989 Market Street, San Francisco, CA 94103

Contact Person
Joe Schuman
Telephone
(415) 782-3232

8. Complete Mailing Address of Headquarters or General Business Office of Publisher *(Not printer)*

Wiley Subscription Services, Inc. 111 River Street, Hoboken, NJ 07030

9. Full Names and Complete Mailing Addresses of Publisher, Editor, and Managing Editor *(Do not leave blank)*
Publisher *(Name and complete mailing address)*

Wiley Subscriptions Services, Inc. A Wiley Company at San Francisco, 989 Market Street, San Francisco, CA 94103-1741

Editor *(Name and complete mailing address)*

Robert Toutkoushian, WW Wright Educ. Bldg Rm 4220, IN. Univ. School of Educ. 201 N. Rose Ave. Bloomington, IN 47405

Managing Editor *(Name and complete mailing address)*

None

10. Owner *(Do not leave blank. If the publication is owned by a corporation, give the name and address of the corporation immediately followed by the names and addresses of all stockholders owning or holding 1 percent or more of the total amount of stock. If not owned by a corporation, give the names and addresses of the individual owners. If owned by a partnership or other unincorporated firm, give its name and address as well as those of each individual owner. If the publication is published by a nonprofit organization, give its name and address.)*

Full Name	Complete Mailing Address
Wiley Subscription Services, Inc.	111 River Street, Hoboken, NJ 07030
(see attached list)	

11. Known Bondholders, Mortgagees, and Other Security Holders Owning or Holding 1 Percent or More of Total Amount of Bonds, Mortgages, or Other Securities. If none, check box ⟶ ☑ None

Full Name	Complete Mailing Address
None	None

12. Tax Status *(For completion by nonprofit organizations authorized to mail at nonprofit rates) (Check one)*
The purpose, function, and nonprofit status of this organization and the exempt status for federal income tax purposes:
☐ Has Not Changed During Preceding 12 Months
☐ Has Changed During Preceding 12 Months *(Publisher must submit explanation of change with this statement)*

13. Publication Title New Directions For Institutional Research	14. Issue Date for Circulation Data Below Summer 2006

15. Extent and Nature of Circulation			Average No. Copies Each Issue During Preceding 12 Months	No. Copies of Single Issue Published Nearest to Filing Date
a. Total Number of Copies *(Net press run)*			1914	1850
b. Paid and/or Requested Circulation	(1)	Paid/Requested Outside-County Mail Subscriptions Stated on Form 3541. *(Include advertiser's proof and exchange copies)*	674	551
	(2)	Paid In-County Subscriptions Stated on Form 3541 *(Include advertiser's proof and exchange copies)*	0	0
	(3)	Sales Through Dealers and Carriers, Street Vendors, Counter Sales, and Other Non-USPS Paid Distribution	0	0
	(4)	Other Classes Mailed Through the USPS	0	0
c. Total Paid and/or Requested Circulation *[Sum of 15b. (1), (2),(3),and (4)]* ▶			674	551
d. Free Distribution by Mail *(Samples, complimentary, and other free)*	(1)	Outside-County as Stated on Form 3541	0	0
	(2)	In-County as Stated on Form 3541	0	0
	(3)	Other Classes Mailed Through the USPS	0	0
e. Free Distribution Outside the Mail *(Carriers or other means)*			46	36
f. Total Free Distribution *(Sum of 15d. and 15e.)* ▶			46	36
g. Total Distribution *(Sum of 15c. and 15f)* ▶			720	587
h. Copies not Distributed			1194	1263
i. Total *(Sum of 15g. and h.)* ▶			1914	1850
j. Percent Paid and/or Requested Circulation *(15c. divided by 15g. times 100)*			94%	94%

16. Publication of Statement of Ownership
☑ Publication required. Will be printed in the ___Winter 2006___ issue of this publication.   ☐ Publication not required.

17. Signature and Title of Editor, Publisher, Business Manager, or Owner

Susan E. Lewis, VP & Publisher - Periodicals

Date
10/01/06

I certify that all information furnished on this form is true and complete. I understand that anyone who furnishes false or misleading information on this form or who omits material or information requested on the form may be subject to criminal sanctions (including fines and imprisonment) and/or civil sanctions (including civil penalties).